bounce back stronger

FINDING **PEACE** AND **PURPOSE** NO MATTER WHAT HAPPENS

Donna Y. Ferris

PRAISE FOR

Bounce Back Stronger

FINDING **PEACE** AND **PURPOSE**
NO MATTER WHAT HAPPENS

"Through Donna Y. Ferris' insightful guide, Bounce Back Stronger, readers are not only invited but empowered to navigate life's setbacks with grace, wisdom, and resilience. Ferris' blend of personal anecdotes, scientific research, and practical exercises provides a roadmap for transforming challenges into opportunities for growth and fulfillment. A must-read for anyone seeking to cultivate resilience and create the life they truly desire."

~ Stephen Cope, Scholar Emeritus Kripalu Center for Yoga and Health,
best-selling author of *Yoga and the Quest for the True Self*

"*Bounce Back Stronger* is a compelling, humorous, and educational essential for any bookshelf. This book is like sharing tea with your closest friend, taking months of therapy, and visiting a sage on the mount all at once. Her practical, high-impact suggestions give you the tools to navigate your personalized journey with resilience, clarity, and confidence."

~ Erin Byron, author of *Safety in the Body*

"Bouncing back from life's challenges is how we build up our capacity for resilience, and Ferris' book offers readers a kind and helping hand in doing so. This book is an ode to small moments every day – knowing and trusting what will unfold when we commit to ourselves for the sake of our healing."

~ Sharon Salzberg, author of *Lovingkindness* and *Real Life*

"The essential practices and perspectives offered in Ferris' work center on a crucial understanding: in order to change our lives, in order to build a more resilient, meaningful, and happier life, we must choose to actively shape our days. Each suggestion offers clear guidance to enable us to navigate difficult moments and take advantage of possibilities in ways that cultivate strength, calm, clarity, and positivity. It is a rich and accessible buffet of choice for anyone!"

~Dr. Maria Sirois, author of
A Short Course in Happiness After Loss (and Other Dark, Difficult Times)

"An honest and authentic sharing of grief and loss, with powerful exercises and suggestions to really help us shift into healing. Love the affirmations! If you're dealing with loss, this is an excellent place to start."

~ Cristina Leeson, international psychic, spiritual leader, and author of
Live in the Light Respect the Dark

ALSO BY

Donna Y. Ferris

Books

We've Got to Stop Meeting Like This

Podcast

Bounce Back Stronger

Bounce Back Stronger

FINDING **PEACE** AND **PURPOSE**
NO MATTER WHAT HAPPENS

by

Donna Y. Ferris

Paperback ISBN: 978-1-7367579-4-9
E-book ISBN: 978-1-7367579-5-6
eBook available
Webpage – donnayferris.com
Bounce Back Stronger playlist can be found on Spotify
Bounce Back Stronger podcast can be found on Apple, Spotify, and all other podcast platforms.

To my Dad

I wish I had this book when we lost you

Table of Contents

1. You Can Do This 1
2. Demystifying Meditation 25
3. Shipwreck 41
4. Survival of the Nurtured 63
5. The Mind Game 79
6. Feelings Inside, Not Expressed 93
7. Resistance is Futile 109
8. Body Wisdom 121
9. Expand Your Bubble 137
10. Remembering the Good 153
11. Create Your Life 169
12. If You Don't Like the Word Faith, Then F*ck It. 185
13. Writing Our Way to Healing 199
14. The Holidays (and Other Tough Days) 215
15. Be a Bumble 225

Acknowledgments 236
Resource List 238
Spotify Playlist 241
Endnotes 242
Excerpt from *The Only Girl in the Room* 244
About the Author 246

"Fearlessness is not the absence of fear. It's the mastery of fear. It's about getting up one more time than we fall down."

Arianna Huffington

Chapter One

You Can Do This

I have a thing for couches.

The one I'm on now is wrapped in snuggly, wide-wale corduroy and cherished because it holds one of my favorite memories.

Weeks after our first date, Mario helped me transport it down four flights of stairs into a moving van. The whole way, we giggled and shouted, "Pivot! Pivot!" just like in that *Friends* episode.

Later, I discovered he had a bad back. Yet he helped me anyway.

Today, I'm nestled in its embrace. Across the room, my 65-pound lab/hound mix, Jake the Wonder Dog, insists it's time for our daily walk with a series of impatient groans from his cozy blue overstuffed chair (more on that later). Nearby, the man who holds my heart sits, tapping away on his laptop. A mug of coffee, crumpled papers, and books surround him. Occasionally, he delights us with a funny meme, song, or line of poetry.

Tranquility and the scent of fresh ground coffee fill the air, creating a sanctuary I'm both aware of and grateful for.

Yet, if someone told me six years ago that I'd be in this moment, I'd have dismissed it as pure fantasy.

* * *

Trudging through the hospice parking lot, the chill from my soaked toes crept through my entire body. I held tightly to my work computer, boombox, two framed family photos, and a glittery picture from my fiancé's daughter as I packed the car.

Mario was still inside.

Nine days since the stroke, and we were finally retreating – but only after he left us first.

Left.

When would I be able to use the word that dripped off the tongues of the hospice nurses? The word they said following his last gasp.

I shivered, but the chill didn't really bother me. For once, being cold felt right.

After stowing the items from Mario's hospice room in the back seat of our seven-passenger SUV, I pulled down my hood and slipped into the driver's seat. My forehead dropped to the steering wheel. I could've stayed like that for hours, but his family could see me as they said their goodbyes a few vehicles away.

I turned on the wipers, carefully backed up the immense vehicle, and quickly saluted Mario's brother as I turned onto Route 273. He was too lost in grief to wave back.

Mario and I traveled this Delaware road many times. But because it was his stomping ground, he always drove. Actually, he drove everything – our life, our relationship, and our family. And I let him do it because he was my world. His unconditional love healed my childhood wounds. I felt safest when I was beside him, even when he could no longer speak.

What was I going to do without him?

Who was I anymore?

I'd been through so much in the last three years. My twenty-plus-year marriage blew up from betrayal. My mother died. I sidelined a high-powered corporate sales career to spend more time with my youngest child and had no idea who I was without it.

Now…I'd lost Mario, the only living person who loved me unconditionally.

The tale of Job comes to mind. (My father was a minister, so there's a biblical reference for everything.) Job was a prosperous, God-fearing man with a large, loving family he adored. Then, suddenly, he faced one tribulation after another. He lost everything.

But what he didn't lose was his faith. He kept going. Again and again.

Still, how much is a person supposed to take?

The SUV leased for our combined family of seven swerved on the sleety roads. I could easily slide into a tree or off a cliff. Would it matter? After all, now it was only me in the car.

A few specks of glitter glimmered on the steering wheel.

The kids.

I lost my dad when I was twenty-five. Our kids were younger.

I needed to keep going, even though I had no interest in the task.

*   *   *

I did continue, and if you're facing a loss, difficulty, or trauma of your own, you can bounce back too.

I'm living proof.

I moved beyond that precarious moment and healed not only from Mario's loss but also from childhood trauma and neglect.

With time, I learned ways to survive, overcome my fears, and became healthy enough to fall in love and marry a kind and caring man who challenges *and* supports me. I learned to be there for my daughters when they needed me in ways I was never taught as a child. Finally, I came to love myself enough to make decisions (like becoming sober) that uplift my life.

Maybe you've just experienced the worst imaginable thing, or are facing your first holiday, birthday, or other special day without a loved one (consider jumping to Chapter Fourteen if that's the case). Maybe you were just downsized in the latest corporate restructuring or lost yourself in another failed relationship.

No matter what it is and how you're feeling, it'll get easier.

You can get through this soul-crushing moment, even though it feels like a thousand-pound iron weight dragging you through the earth. You can even turn it into a triumph that will open your heart to more than you ever imagined.

How do I know?

Soon after my fiancé died, my youngest child declared in a text that they were non-binary, and over the next two years, they transitioned to a new gender.

As a result of the losses and lessons I learned in the prior three years when I got that text, I was able to focus less on how it would affect me and more on how hard it was for her to live in a body that didn't feel like hers. This was a victory because the person I was before would have made the entire situation about how it affected me.

It may be hard to believe, but because of these shifts in me, I'm (mostly) grateful for what I've experienced. It helped me remember who I am (a mother who puts her children's needs first) and solidified what matters (my children's happiness way more than my own ego). It also gave me the tools to find peace no matter the situation (especially helpful in business and parenting) as well as my life purpose.

Because our time on earth is too short to waste.

And even though I may not succeed in staying out of the trance of fear, despair, and rumination each day, I now have the awareness and fortitude to fail, bounce back, and try over and over again.

I tell you this because many times, when we're facing difficulty, we can't do the hard work of healing – especially if we were never taught to love ourselves. Into adulthood, my mother called me selfish whenever I advocated for myself, but now, I know that's because she heard the same thing when she was a child.

A Gateway to a New Way of Living

If you're thinking that I was able to bounce back because there's something special about me, nothing could be further from the truth.

The only thing that might be a little different is that I've loved wisdom philosophy since I was a kid. Maybe because I adored my dad, and we always hid from my mother in his study. As he wrote his sermons, I would read his Bible commentaries. In middle school, my parents took me on a mission trip to India. There were no TVs, so to pass the time, I read books of Indian fables, most religiously based. After my dad died, I started reading more secular works like *The Four Agreements* and *A Course in Miracles*. Then I discovered *The*

Tao of Pooh, Breakfast with Buddha, and *Zen for Dummies,* which eventually led me to enroll in a one-year yoga teacher training program weeks before the betrayal that led to my divorce (more on that in Chapter Twelve).

Yoga training and its Eastern philosophy focus was a gateway to a new way of living. It gave me an awareness of the interplay between body, mind, and spirit that helped me discover the impact of energy on our lives and those who have left us. I found it so grounding that I doubled down and started a three-year yoga therapy certification.

Because of the loss of my marriage – and the deaths of my mother and fiancé that followed – I was broken *and* open enough to listen. We humans rarely change for the better when things are good. We're inclined only to do it when things are difficult, when our pain becomes so great that we're forced from our comfort zone to seek relief. We want something, anything that works.

Through these experiences and study, I developed a process to help me overcome challenging times – to master life changes with as much grace as possible and not lose myself when the ground shifts and churns.

This book shares this process along with activities to support your healing. The chapters are laid out in an order that is chronological and logical to me, but feel free to start with any chapter that appeals to you.

Only you know what is best for you.

Please know this is an ongoing learning practice, which is part of the reason I started the *Bounce Back Stronger* podcast – to continue learning from others on this path.

Because change doesn't stop. Since the events I've already

mentioned, the pandemic hit, causing me to face a drinking problem. During that time, I supported several loved ones who attempted suicide, stemming from the effects of pandemic isolation and loneliness (which is it's own epidemic – more on that later). Most recently, like many of us, I've been dealing with the constant uncertainty of the workforce due to systemic trends, including remote work and the career impacts of new technology like artificial intelligence.

Each time, I applied the tools in this book and added to them, using my experiences and what I learned from others.

As a result, I've been able to bounce back stronger and find peace and determination each time, and I'm hopeful you will be able to do the same.

That said, not everything I share here will resonate with you. So take what works, and set aside the rest (maybe a seed will take root and offer inspiration later). Just remember you can get through this and thrive in spite of it (or perhaps even *because* of it). You may even know the right answers now – you just need the confidence to act on them.

The Science of Resilience

Maybe the thought of bouncing back is too much – a concept you can't conceive. You're barely making it through today.

I've been there. And I'm a skeptic and typically reject things before I accept them.

Because of this, I find science helpful in turning resistance into acceptance.

This brings us to the scientific research of Dr. Steven Southwick, a renowned expert in the field of psychology and neuroscience from Yale (he died in 2022). He worked at the National Center for PTSD of the US Department of Veteran's Affairs and focused primarily on how people become resilient after traumatization. His life work sheds light on how our brains can not only adapt to difficulty but can also heal.

Where does his research begin? Neuroplasticity – which refers to the brain's remarkable ability to adapt and reorganize itself. When we face adversity or trauma, our brains can form new neural connections and pathways, enabling us to learn, grow, and ultimately recover.

Whenever I hear this idea of neural connections, I think of that *Star Trek: The Next Generation* episode (yes – I'm a Trekkie) when the artificial intelligence named Data lost one of his closest friends. Although he couldn't actually feel anything, he described losing the person as having a well-worn path that is no longer accessible. He sorely missed having that routine in his processing completed.

Maybe not how you think about loss. But it might be helpful to look at it that way. When our relationships are disrupted by loss, our brains are knocked off their usual track. But like a computer, Dr. Southwick found that our brains can rewire themselves. They are not fixed forever – we can develop new pathways to help us cope. That is what this book is about – identifying ways to reprogram ourselves to find peace and purpose no matter what happens (for more on this topic, listen to Episode 2 of my podcast *Bounce Back Stronger*[1]).

"A new science called neuroaesthetics has discovered that looking at beautiful things can actually boost our mood and help us navigate life changes by creating more neural connections in our brains."

Donna Y. Ferris

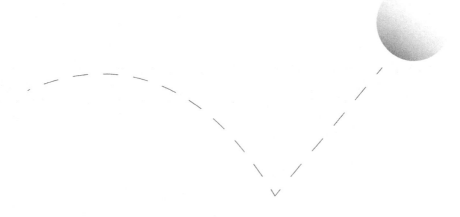

What is Your Why?

One of the best lessons I've learned along my journey is that you need a reason to bounce back. For me, it was my kids.

With that in mind, turn to the back of this chapter to find the blank lined pages and write the word "Why" at the top of the first page. Start a ten-minute timer on your phone, and write whatever comes to mind. (There are no wrong answers.)

If the blank page is overwhelming, here are some ideas:

- **MEANINGFUL RELATIONSHIPS** – Is there a "who" you want to be there for, such as your children, parents, partner, or dog/cat?

- **LIFE PURPOSE –** Is there more you want to do in your life, or do you want to make an impact on the world? You might have a life purpose or a philanthropic pursuit. (We'll discuss this further in Chapter 11.)

- **PERSONAL GROWTH –** Do you value learning? Is there something you can discover from what you're going through? A certificate or degree you want to earn?

- **RESILIENCE –** Do you have grit or feel compelled to prove to yourself (and others) that you can overcome challenges and adversity?

- **CORE BELIEFS –** What do you believe is most important? Your family, your participation in a religious organization or charity, your impact on a neighborhood, school, or other social group? Might that be your why?

- **HOW IS BEING ALIVE A GIFT?** Think how tough it is to be born and how heartbreaking it is to lose someone. With that in mind, every day we're alive is something to be grateful for (Mario and I were the same age, so every year I keep living feels like a special bonus). What blessings do you see in your life today - it could be as small as having milk that is unexpired for your morning coffee or as big as getting a friendly text from a friend or family member.

Post this list somewhere that you can see it daily, or keep a screenshot of it or your loved ones on your phone or by your bedside.

Find Your Team

Another essential support on this journey is your "healing team." First, I recommend finding a psychologist and/or psychiatrist (if you don't already have one) because this book is certainly not a replacement for therapy or medical treatment. It contains what worked for me, but everyone's journey is different. Mine included at least bi-weekly calls to my therapist.

Finding a mental health professional can be challenging, so "date" several before you commit. Ask your insurance company and a medical professional you trust for recommendations, and tell your regular medical doctor what you're going through. They may prescribe medication that will be helpful for your healing or refer you to a psychiatrist for that purpose.

I also suggest you find other wellness professionals, including life coaches, yoga therapists, massage therapists, Reiki Masters, and/or EFT (Emotional Freedom Technique) professionals. They may be able to help you manage the non-clinical aspects of what you are going through. This life struggle affects not only your mind but your body, soul, and energy field, too. You also might consult a minister, rabbi, or other religious professional to support you on the spiritual aspects of your journey.

The last members of your healing team are people or groups who have also gone through something difficult and had a positive outcome. They haven't just survived but thrived in a genuine, achievable way. They may be the only people in your life who can understand your feelings – and this is comforting, grounding, and healing. These might include groups that address grief, addiction, career transitions, or women's issues.

Other Tools and How to Use This Book

This book is not meant to be read in one sitting. It's meant to be taken a chapter at a time. I hope you will try on the ideas in the chapters to see how they fit. Write how they make you feel. Maybe read a chapter day by day, week by week, or use whatever cadence makes sense to give you time to explore the content and related tools, which include:

 JOURNALING. Each chapter of this book will have a journaling prompt. You may be thinking, "I've tried journaling before, and it doesn't work for me." Please try again. I've included some blank lined pages after each chapter to get you started. If you need more pages, go online or to a nearby bookstore to pick out a pretty journal or notebook that speaks to you today. When we're going through difficult times, we feel emotional energy, and one of the best ways to harness and let energy flow through us is with a creative activity like journaling (drawing works, too). Witnessing our stories through some artistic activity lets us see them more clearly and reshape them. Only we have the power to turn our stories of despair into uplifting tales of resilience.

MEDITATION – Every chapter after this one includes a link to a related meditation recording (one even has a yoga practice). If you're new to meditation, the next chapter will explain why this activity is crucial for this journey.

 AFFIRMATIONS – Each chapter also has a list of affirmations you can write down on a sticky note at your desk or bedside, use as a mantra, or you can take a picture of them to use as wallpaper for your phone. These affirmations provide reframing opportunities to lift you during challenging moments. One affirmation is also captured on a coloring page at the end of each chapter in case you love to color (like me). At the end of this chapter is an additional calendar coloring page in case it's helpful to color in every day you are on this journey. All of the coloring pages in this book have been put together in a PDF book. To receive a copy of this PDF please email me at donna@donnayferris.com or visit my website donnayferris.com to access it.

GRATITUDE PRACTICE – It's easy to wallow when we're going through difficult times, which makes it hard to feel grateful for anything. But it's challenging to find joy if you can't appreciate what you have. So get out your phone or go to your work calendar to schedule three recurring five-minute gratitude timeouts each day. Write down your three things in your journaling pages. Or you can jot them down on pieces of paper and store them in a mason jar or box – so you can pull them out when you need them.

FOLLOW THE COLOR AND CRYSTAL GUIDANCE – Feelings about loss and change are emotional energy. To support managing the ebb and flow of this energy, I've included information on which energy chakras are relevant to each chapter; please ignore them if you feel uncomfortable with this information. But if you feel drawn to this idea, try working with the colors and crystals. Consider wearing a chakra color or carrying a related crystal in your pocket. Notice what happens and capture any outcomes in your journaling pages.

 PLANT A SEED – LITERALLY! Go to your local hardware store, pick up a package of tomato seeds or flowers you like, and plant them. Use pots indoors if the weather is unfavorable or outdoors if feasible. Follow the directions, and notice how a little water and sunshine can make anything grow, including you. You can also buy a potted plant if it's easier. Make sure to try this one because we will refer back to it later.

 START A SUNRISE AND/OR SUNSET PRACTICE – For a week (and, if possible, longer), commit to observing the sunrise and/or sunset each day. Every sunrise and sunset differs depending on the weather, time of year, and positions of the planets and stars. This practice reminds us that every day offers a stunning new start, and every night can be let go of with grace and wonder.

LOOK TO DO SOMETHING THAT FILLS YOUR HEART WITH AWE – If the sunrise/sunset practice above isn't possible, seek to do at least one thing each week that fills your heart with awe. A new science called neuroaesthetics[2] has discovered that looking at beautiful things can actually boost our mood and help us navigate life changes by creating more neural connections in our brains. With that in mind, go to a museum, local botanical garden, or concert. Visit a beach or lake, plan a trip somewhere you've always wanted to go, or attend a local fair or event. Do something that lifts you from the routine and reminds you how unbelievably precious and gorgeous life is.

 DO SOMETHING FOR SOMEONE ELSE – If you're up for it, engaging in acts of kindness during tough times can create a positive distraction that temporarily alleviates emotional pain. These efforts also trigger the release of feel-good neurotransmitters, such as serotonin and dopamine, contributing to a sense of happiness. Finally, these activities can empower us and give us greater control over our circumstances. Some of my favorite ways to do for others are volunteering at animal rescues, organizing drives for hospital women's clinics or domestic violence centers, and giving food to the local food bank. (Please note that if this feels like too much, honor those feelings.)

 CONNECT THROUGH AN EVENT OR LISTEN TO THE BOUNCE BACK STRONGER PODCAST – Visit donnayferris.com/events or email me at donna@donnayferris.com for information on upcoming workshops, retreats, or speaking events. This book includes what I have learned so far about resilience. For ongoing learnings, tune into the weekly *Bounce Back Stronger* podcast, which shares inspiring stories of how others have overcome difficulty and tools that can help; search for it wherever you listen to podcasts. Also, feel free to email me and just say hello. I love to hear from readers.

Again, please take your time with each chapter. Maybe do the meditation a few times. Follow the journaling prompt. Say the affirmations and see if one suits you. Complete the coloring page. Go see a sunset. Visit a spiritual energy store and pick up the crystals (maybe an Oracle card deck while you are there). Notice what speaks to you from the chapter. Know that there are no wrong answers – and breathe in that you already know what is best for you.

You Can Get Through This

Finally, please know you can get through this. If I can, I truly believe you can. Befriending your mind through meditation is an essential part of the how. Read on to the next chapter to find out why.

Journaling Exercise

Go to your journaling pages and write down a sentence or two (or more) on the following prompts:

- **WHY? –** What is driving you to bounce back from this setback? Revisit this discussion earlier in the chapter for suggestions if it's helpful.

- **WHO? –** Who is in my corner to help me get through this? Support can come from a psychologist, medical doctor, life coach, minister/priest/chaplain, holistic practitioner, grief or other support groups. Maybe reach out to one or more of them this week.

- **GRATITUDE –** Write three things you are grateful for today, and schedule your three 5-minute gratitude breaks on your phone or work calendar.

Meditation Practice

Read the next chapter, and visit donnayferris.com/meditation. Pick one of the meditations that appeals to you today. Trust that the Universe / God is with you, and you will choose the right one. Write down the meditation you picked in your journaling pages (we will revisit this later).

Affirmations

- I can endure and survive this loss.
- It's okay to take care of myself while I grieve.
- Every one of my feelings is important.
- Despite this loss, there are things to be grateful for.
- I am not alone; everyone experiences loss.
- There are many reasons to keep going.
- Love never dies.
- I am stronger than I know.
- It is healthy and proper to feel and embrace happiness when it comes.
- Everything will be okay.

"We don't meditate
to get better at meditating;
we meditate to
get better at life."

Sharon Salzberg

Chapter Two

Demystifying Meditation

It was the first Thanksgiving after my divorce – a whirlwind that took four and a half months from cheating discovery to final decree.

I guess we both wanted out.

My ex insisted on taking the kids to Florida to see his mother for Turkey Day – an annual tradition that I was uninvited from. I was relieved not to go on the trip *and* upset because it was the first time I would not spend this holiday with my kids.

Looking around my favorite yoga studio's website, I found a notice for a restoration yoga class. I'd never taken one. I didn't even know what it was.

But who doesn't want to feel restored?

As I entered the purple room with bamboo floors, everyone was pulling bolsters and blankets to their mats. Wimps. I don't need any stinking props. I'd just turned fifty-one. Darned if I would give myself the support of a pillow or blanket. I needed to prove to everyone (and myself) that my body was still fierce and capable.

The teacher started her playlist. Ugh. No words. Only instrumentals with flutes, Tibetan bowls, and new-age music. I hoped I wouldn't fall asleep.

She explained that the seventy-five-minute class would involve a series of ten to fifteen propped postures that we would hold for up to five minutes each.

Five minutes? How in the world would I do that?

During each posture, she encouraged us to hold a conversation between our bodies and minds. And she promised to give suggestions for meditation practice.

At the "M" word, I should have bolted. There's no way I would have signed up if I'd known meditation was involved.

I'd just started yoga teacher training and didn't yet comprehend that the Savasana at the end of yoga classes was meditation. I just thought it was the calming reward for all the sweating and pain of the preceding class – one of the few times I could stand being still.

She began the practice and dropped us into our first pose – seated butterfly with blocks under each knee. This was a pose I could easily perform. I grabbed my toes and settled in.

Before long, the discomfort in my hips became impossible to ignore. It was too early to start with this pose or hold it for any length of time. "How silly she is," I thought. "She might injure someone! Maybe I should intervene?"

But as I looked around the room, the other students had their eyes closed, and their faces were soft. Some even glowed. One woman was fidgeting in the front row, but the teacher quickly brought a blanket to place under her bum, and she settled down.

Not me. My mind was racing, thinking how difficult this was, how I'd rather be with my kids, and why had my husband ruined everything by cheating? The teacher kept moving us to other positions and even gave us props to withstand them, but it was torture. I had no tools to help me sit with my thoughts, and after the class felt anything but restored. I vowed never to go to a class like that again and believed meditation would never be something I could make routine.

It took three more years for me to sign up willingly for meditation training. Yes, I took meditation classes as part of my yoga teacher and yoga therapy certifications, but none of them voluntarily.

It wasn't until Mario died that I thought meditation could help me find peace. . . maybe. But honestly, the only reason I took the training was because my yoga "crush," Stephen Cope, was the co-leader.

The other teacher? Sharon Salzberg, the mother of Loving Kindness meditation.

Yuck. Sounded like BS.

Growing up in abuse, I didn't have any context for loving-kindness. It sounded like Bhakti (heart-centered) nonsense.

During our first session, Salzberg asked if anyone could clear their mind for two minutes. Almost everyone raised their hands. I did, too. Then she proceeded to ask about other lengths of time. Five minutes, twenty minutes, forty-five minutes. By the time she got to an hour, there were no hands raised.

Then, she said, "I can only keep my mind clear for four breaths."

Whaaaaat? I need to get my money back! Here's this meditation guru I paid good money to see, and she can't keep it together in meditation for more than four breaths?

Salzberg shared that no one can clear their mind for longer than that. Our minds are constantly drifting to rumination. The purpose of meditation is to train our thoughts to return to the breath. To catch unhelpful thinking and remind us of our divine selves again and again. It's possible only with practice.

So, it wasn't just me. No one can do this.

I had it all wrong, which doesn't mean the teachers before were incompetent. I just wasn't ready to hear what they had to say. It took Salzberg's simple admission to get me out of my way. She demystified the practice for me.

It may be the most valuable gift anyone ever gave me.

It Just Takes a Little Practice

That was in 2018, and I've been meditating regularly ever since. It took another six months to commit to a daily five-minute practice. And today? My practice is at least fifteen minutes in the morning (usually with yoga), plus a few gratitude meditation "snacks" (where I identify at least one thing I'm grateful for) to break me out of my ruminating or worrying trance during the day. At night, I do a few stretching moves and meditate for at least ten breaths before bed.

At first, meditation was all about giving me peace and a break from my thoughts. Over time, the practice grew into befriending my mind and noticing and working with my thoughts rather than clearing them.

Meditation has helped me survive and thrive through the deaths of loved ones, the transition of my daughter, multiple corporate reorganizations, and other challenges. It grounded me as I wrote the most harrowing scenes in my memoir. I do not write, post on social media, or talk to my husband or family without meditating first.

I even use it at work. If I have a big meeting, I drop a black obsidian crystal in my palm and take five minutes beforehand to listen to a guided meditation or take ten to fifteen slow breaths. This practice calms my nervous system and helps me be at my best.

I also lead a weekly fifteen-minute centering practice for others on this path. We've supported each other through corporate restructurings, the pandemic, and personal difficulties. I value these interactions as much as those with my family and close friends.

Why Should You Meditate?

But enough about me. Why should you commit to a meditation practice – especially now?

Studies[3] have shown that regular meditation can improve focus and attention, control anxiety, improve sleep, promote brain health, and support recovery from addiction.

The practice is particularly helpful when going through difficult times. It can give us a break from our torrential, spinning thoughts that can career from past failures to imagined future tragedies. It also helps us regulate our emotions.

All quite helpful when navigating loss and change.

What About Prayer?

Before we leave this chapter and launch into the rest, it might be helpful to contrast the differences between prayer and meditation, as they are complementary rather than interchangeable.

Simply put, prayer is communicating with and requesting guidance and support from a higher power, while meditation is befriending our minds to provide calm, reduce stress, enhance self-awareness, and improve concentration.

Both may lead to a connection with a higher power, but prayer is communication with a higher being – talking, listening, thinking, praising, and thanking, while meditation is focused on working with our thoughts to create calm (which may also lead to a connection with the universe or higher powers).

During difficult times, both are incredibly helpful.

For example, I might pray to a higher power to bring peace and healing to my friend who is suffering from cancer and meditate with her to reduce stress and calm her before treatments.

No One Way to Meditate

After every chapter of this book, you will be prompted to listen to a short, free, recorded meditation at donnayferris.com/meditations. Here are some of the types we will explore:

- **MINDFULNESS MEDITATION** – Noticing the breath, sounds, sights, smells, touches, and tastes in this moment allows the rest of the world to fall away. Every moment holds the transformative power to start anew.

- **WALKING MEDITATION** – Taking a walk in nature and focusing solely on what is experienced with each footfall can be calming and healing.

- **VISUALIZATION MEDITATION** – Imagining a beautiful place that makes you happy or a future you want to manifest.

- **LOVING KINDNESS MEDITATION** – This practice uses four simple phrases (like the ones below) and applies them to ourselves, others, and all beings:

  - **MAY YOU BE HAPPY.**
  - **MAY YOU BE HEALTHY.**
  - **MAY YOU BE SAFE.**
  - **MAY YOU LIVE WITH EASE.**

- **MANTRA MEDITATION** – This practice focuses on one phrase or affirmation as a pathway to universal connection. Transcendental meditation uses this technique.

It's a Practice, Not a Performance

Be kind to yourself. Meditation is a practice, not a performance. It's normal for the mind to wander during meditation. Instead of being critical when this happens, gently guide your focus to your chosen anchor, such as the breath or a mantra. To reinforce the practice, note any difference between the days you meditate and those you don't in your journaling pages.

Now, with meditation in your toolkit and your team by your side, it's time to turn to the next chapter of our journey, where we look at what happens in our bodies and minds when faced with a sudden loss or change – and some simple proven ways to navigate those times.

Journaling Exercise

How can you fit meditation into your day? Identify a five-to-ten-minute period and commit to it for one week. Doing it first thing in the morning typically ensures it happens, and it's always helpful to fit in some deep breaths when waiting in lines or while your computer or a video call boots up. Keep track of each day you meditate for the next month, and note if your mood, ability to manage stress or general happiness changed as a result.

"It's normal for the mind to wander during meditation. Instead of being critical when this happens, gently guide your focus to your chosen anchor, such as the breath or a mantra."

Donna Y. Ferris

Meditation

Try A Short Mindfulness Practice from the donnayferris.com/ meditations page (this meditation is also *Bounce Back Stronger* podcast episode 4).

Crown Chakra, Color, and Crystals

The crown chakra is the seventh and highest energy center and is located at the top of the head. Symbolized by the color violet or white, this chakra represents spiritual connection, divine consciousness, and enlightenment. It serves as the gateway to higher states of awareness and understanding. Crystals such as amethyst, clear quartz, and selenite are often used to balance and activate the crown chakra.

Affirmations

I am peaceful.

Peace is as close as a breath.

I can find time for myself and my needs.

Today, I choose to live in the moment.

All my thoughts are okay.

I inhale peace and harmony. I exhale stress and worries.

I can always take deep breaths.

I can handle what comes my way.

My meditation practice is getting better by the day.

My mind and body heal with each breath.

"I still miss those I loved who are no longer with me, but I find I am grateful for having loved them.
The gratitude has finally conquered the loss."

Rita Mae Brown

Chapter Three

Shipwreck

When I saw our old dog, Samson, on the floor, I knew the dreaded decision was here.

Our younger pup, Jake, jumped off the couch and blocked my path. I bent down, and he pushed his nose into my face. Whining is his favorite form of communication, but this raspy, mournful sound was new.

Uncharacteristically, Samson stayed where he was. He usually greeted me with his Irish setter dance of excitement. But today, he sat still, shaking. When I hugged him, he didn't move. I scurried to bring a water bowl to his feet, but for the first time, he refused to drink.

He'd been declining for almost a year, but that didn't make this easier. Especially since we'd lost our other senior dog, Yogi, only seven months before.

We went to the vet and discussed his deterioration. After some deliberation, we decided to help him transition. An hour later, my husband held him as he fell asleep.

Then he was gone.

We left the vet with only his collar, but the hole in our hearts was infinitely more expansive than the body it once encircled.

When we returned home, the quiet in the house was deafening.

Samson's loss was like a shipwreck, and our grief had us struggling to keep our heads above water.

Don't do it alone

Feelings of shock in response to loss can last for days, weeks, or months. The body steps in and won't let us feel the full extent of our sorrow at first because we can't stand it.

It can be hard to do anything – even trips to the grocery store or post office feel impossible. We forget what we're doing midway through and find ourselves seeing lost loved ones in crowds – only to be shocked again they are gone.

This is normal.

In the early days of grief, it helps to reach out to our support network (therapists, close friends, spiritual guides), let our boss know we're going through something difficult (and take bereavement or sick leave if appropriate and available), and then place a blanket of self-care over our lives.

We need to care for ourselves first to make the next best move, the next one, and the next. Even though our instincts might push us in other directions.

Emergency Self-Care List

Depending upon the magnitude of the loss, we may unconsciously forgo healthy habits with regard to sleep, hydrating, or eating. We might turn to addictive behaviors (alcohol, drugs, gambling, shopping) to numb the pain. We may withdraw from others and think we are better off not living. If you're worried you could become sad enough to harm yourself, develop a plan with your therapist for what you will do when that happens, which may include going to a nearby emergency room or dialing 911 for help (or 988 for the suicide hotline).

It can also be helpful to notice if you are hungry, angry, lonely, or tired (also known as the acronym "HALT"). If one of these feelings applies, consider eating and writing down your feelings (and/or talking with your therapist). It is also good to establish a healthy sleep routine by doing the following:

- **DESIGNATE** a place for sleep only, with no working in that space.
- **REFRAIN** from eating or consuming alcohol three hours before bed. Our bodies need time overnight to process our food and rejuvenate. Eating or drinking too close to bed can interrupt these processes.
- **PUT AWAY** phones a half hour before bedtime. The phone's blue light messes up our biological clock, and doomscrolling doesn't help either (putting the phone away early really helps me).
- **KEEP** the phone out of reach and face down. Mine sits more than an arm's length from me and is turned face down so my sleep isn't disturbed by the light of middle-of-the-night messaging.

- **START** a gratitude practice. Brené Brown found in her studies[4] that people who call themselves joyful have some kind of gratitude practice. Studies[5] have shown that writing down even three things we are grateful for can have an incredibly positive effect on our lives.
- **CREATE** a bedtime ritual. Mine is writing down what I'm grateful for (see above), listing the actions I can do to serve my purpose the next day, meditating, and reading a book that isn't stimulating.
- **WAKE UP** the next day and notice how you feel. Are you exhausted or anxious? Is your face puffy? Note what you did or consumed the night before. How does all that drinking, eating, exercising, or shopping make you feel in the morning? Make adjustments in your nightly routine to reflect what you've learned.

It also helps to keep a short list of emergency self-care activities. We will discuss the benefits of a more routine self-nurturing practice in the next chapter, but in the early days, we need Band-Aid activities like:

- **CALL A THERAPIST**, loved one, or friend
- **TAKE A WALK** outside or into another room
- **LISTEN TO HAPPY MUSIC** (see the playlist in the back of this book. Also, I highly recommend the Al Jarreau playlist on Pandora – more on that here[6]).
- **HYDRATE**
- **COMMIT TO FOODS** that support mental health (check out this episode[7] of *The Doctor's Kitchen* podcast with Dr. Rupy).

- **GARDEN**
- **PUT SOOTHING** skin lotion all over your body.
- **WORK ON A PUZZLE**
- **WATCH FUNNY SITCOMS** or movies

Take "Forgetting" Breaks

To help us get through Samson's loss, we re-watched the TV show *Ted Lasso* (this was probably our third go-round). It's funny and shares wisdom for navigating change. One of my favorite scenes is when Ted suggests a player "be like a goldfish" when handling a disappointment. He says goldfish have a memory of only ten seconds.

Similarly, giving ourselves brief "forgetting" breaks from loss can be helpful. Even changing rooms or going outside can reduce the intensity of emotional energy. Try getting a cup of tea, wiggling toes and fingers, or taking ten deep breaths. These peaceful timeouts allow us to rest and imagine a life where grief doesn't dominate every minute – a break from the force of our feelings so that we can let our minds be in the moment rather than racing ahead or behind.

With these pauses, we can better handle the successive grief waves as they come. We may feel like we're drowning, but we can keep our heads above water. Think of yourself as a master surfer who rides the big waves of emotion when they come.

And remember, no feeling lasts forever, no matter how difficult it may be.

Not All Losses Are the Same

The loss of a dog or someone close to us is just one of the more *impactful* events we have to bounce back from. Here are some others:

- Divorce
- Loss of a job
- Corporate reorganization
- Moving (downsizing or moving offices count)
- Personal injury or disease
- Retirement
- Drug or alcohol addiction
- Global unrest
- Disaster

I call these *impactful* losses because when they happen, we have to make significant changes that may include modifications in:

- Life plans
- Address and utilities
- Locks
- Jobs or career
- New bosses
- Emergency contacts
- Medical or veterinary doctors
- Beneficiaries
- Tax filings
- Banking and investment accounts

Changes like these can have an impact, too:
- Post-pregnancy
- Business readjustment
- Change in financial state
- Change to a different line of work
- Change in frequency of arguments in a close relationship
- Major mortgage
- Child leaving home
- Beginning or end of school

Of course, taking on a major mortgage isn't devastating like the death of a loved one, but it disrupts our finances, taxes, and travel prospects as every aspect of how we view money will change.

Even positive events like being a new mother can cause negative feelings if we don't give ourselves a break (or discuss it with a mental health or medical professional). Especially if other events from the lists above are happening simultaneously (which many are surprised to find). Yet, we tend to try to muscle through – and may experience some depression and resentment as a result. Then, we feel guilty or think we shouldn't feel that way.

Don't Should All Over Yourself

Someone once told me that guilt is a wasted emotion and that I should stop "shoulding" all over myself. Anyone who loves us would never want us to feel guilty or regretful about our actions toward them.

But loss and change bring up these uncomfortable feelings (and many more), and they are all valid.

Most of us aren't taught how to handle the range of our feelings – and might only have seen anger, sadness, and fear modeled. But not giving ourselves grace for our feelings can leave us feeling guilty and bad about ourselves – and we can get stuck there.

Feelings aren't scary – we can have them without acting on them. In fact, once we are aware of our painful feelings, we can see them as clues that a timeout of self-care and self-love is needed (more on this in Chapter Six).

Once we realize what is happening, the next step is ours to take.

The Only Thing We Can Count On is Change

Ever feel like once you get through "this thing," everything will be easier? Or that time will heal the pain.

But changes never end. There is always another one.

And time does not magically heal wounds – every new loss we experience re-triggers all our previous losses. So, we cannot rely on the passing of time to undo our pain.

That's why we need to get to a place where change doesn't unravel us. We need to be able to recover no matter what happens. In fact, this change you're going through may be a key growth catalyst on your journey. (If this is tough to hear right now, that's okay. Honor those feelings and also know that it is possible.)

When my grandfather died more than forty years ago, a friend gave me the book *How to Survive the Loss of a Love*. I loved that book and still recommend it.

But now, surviving is not enough. I believe we can transform our reactions to change. Accept rather than resist. See each trial as an opportunity – not to survive, but thrive.

We must become more than what happens to us.

If that feels like too much right now, I understand. The loss is too raw, the change overwhelming. You may still be in reaction mode. Maybe a discussion of normal reactions to change will help. Try to give yourself some grace, grab a cup of tea, light a candle, and read on.

Reactions to Change

We can't help how we react to change. It's instinct kicking in. Typically, we face change or loss with these responses:

- **FIGHT** – resistance and anger.
- **FLIGHT** – running away or denying.
- **FREEZE** – paralyzed, unable to move forward. We can get stuck here and never leave. This is where PTSD lives in the body and mind.
- **FAWN** – trying to make it all better for everyone.

You might be familiar with the first three, but "fawn" may be new. Fawn is the act of trying to make everything okay. This is for the over-functioners – those who bounce into high gear at the sign

"We must become more than what happens to us."

Donna Y. Ferris

of difficulty. It's a coping mechanism as unhealthy as the first three when we struggle to take back control. We might be better off accepting that we have none.

Fawn is my go-to reaction. When Mario died, I started cleaning the house and making arrangements for the family to visit – and the night of his funeral was spent managing a family crisis for a loved one. When I finally got into a warm bath, the water suddenly stopped because someone had plugged up a toilet, and they had to shut off the water to the house to prevent flooding.

And, of course, they all came to find me in my nakedness. I'd lost a man who meant everything, yet everyone looked to me to solve their problems.

This is my fault. I didn't let on how much I was suffering. I was still in take-no-prisoners mode on the outside, even though I was sinking slowly into a black hole.

When we do this, we rob those around us of the opportunity to grow and learn how to care for us (and others), and we keep ourselves from the joy of realizing we can let that happen

We *can* be taken care of instead of doing it all for everyone else.

Yes, everything might not be exactly as we desire – but who the hell cares (especially now)? Letting go of perfection and letting life *flow* a bit more may be precisely what we need.

Stages of Grief

It might be helpful here to share some understanding of the five stages of grief as Kubler-Ross and Kessler[8] describe them. They are:

- **DENIAL –** This change or loss is too hard to take. We push it away until we can deal with it.
- **ANGER –** We may get furious about it. Why me? We may even get mad at the person who caused the pain – even if they're dead.
- **BARGAINING –** We bargain with the situation. For example: "If I do such and such, it won't hurt so much."
- **DEPRESSION –** This is when it all sinks in, and depression hits. We feel the loss and sometimes get stuck and wallow in it. (I am a great wallower, by the way.)
- **ACCEPTANCE –** Ding, ding, ding! The quicker we get from the initial loss to acceptance of what has occurred, the quicker we can move on and integrate it into our lives.

Please note that grief phases can happen in a different order or repeat. Very few people go straight to acceptance, and the benefit of knowing the stages and process is awareness. The sooner you realize you're in one of these stages, the sooner you can travel through and accept what is happening.

But that doesn't mean you should muscle through because dealing with change and loss is like converting energy in physics. Energy doesn't go away. Neither does grief. It has to be harnessed and transformed somehow by writing about it, talking to someone, taking action, and lots and lots of self-care.

Disrupting Our Homeostasis

Why do we react to change and loss so *viscerally*? Our homeostasis or life equilibrium is disrupted. Changes trigger basic instincts developed by our prehistoric caveperson ancestors to survive, including:

- Fear of being wrong or lazy
- Fear of being unloved or unwanted
- Fear of being worthless or disrespected
- Fear of meaninglessness
- Fear of not knowing
- Fear of chaos
- Fear of deprivation
- Fear of being controlled
- Fear of being confronted

Even though we're no longer part of a prehistoric tribe and no longer need to be connected to get access to shelter and food, these fears trigger us as if we were still facing life-and-death situations. We fall into a trance where feeling unloved, unwanted, or left behind makes us feel like we will die. Our bodies may physically react, even when we're perfectly safe.

Meditation Helps

What is the best way to get ourselves out of this automatic response? A regular meditation practice. As noted in the last chapter, befriending our minds through meditation allows us to see when our brains are off track.

When we practice making friends with our minds, we note when we are ruminating and can say, "Thank you so much, body and mind, for trying to save me and keep me safe. But I'm okay."

This trance is triggered all the time. A recent Harvard study[9] says that our minds wander 46 percent of the time. With meditation practice, we can see this happening and remember who we aspire to be – instead of acting on our fears, needs, and wants.

Uncertainty and Identity

Another reason changes hit us so hard is they create tremendous uncertainty and loss of identity. My sense of identity changes when my children go to school, my job changes, or when I retire. I'm uncertain of who I am in this new phase.

Maybe the trick is not to get stuck in our perception of who we are. Instead, we can seek to build awareness and tolerance of what is happening inside and out. Then, we can apply an energy timeout to rest our body and nervous system through meditation or some other activity from our personal emergency list.

And it may be helpful to realize that we take on personas in life – and we can change them at any time. There is a persona of grief – which we may inhabit to such an extent that we don't allow any other feelings (including happiness) to emerge when they do. You can be desperately sad to lose someone and elated to see friends and family at their funeral. (More on personas in Chapter Five.)

Don't deny *any* joyful feelings. They are gifts from the divine.

Why It's Important to Try?

As we wrap up this chapter, let's look at why moving through the grief, sorrow, and hardship we experience is essential. Several studies[10] show that if we don't address and work through traumatic events, we can experience negative impacts to our physical health. As mentioned, each time we encounter a new loss, we touch base with every other loss we've experienced. So it's important to process each one because if we don't, it will come back again.

The body is eavesdropping on everything we think, and if we tell our body we don't want to live anymore because of a loss or that our heart is irreparably broken, it will listen.

We speak things into being, so look for and give yourself experiences that stimulate happy thoughts. Happiness is hard in the early days of grief, but little moments of nurturing allow us to build on them. Even if it's only a *Ted Lasso* episode about goldfish. You've got nothing to lose and everything to gain.

As we prepare to move on, the journaling exercise that follows may be the most important thing you (and your loved ones) can do. I hope you will take the time to complete it.

Journaling Exercise

Write down at least five emergency self-care activities. Some of mine are:

- Call my therapist.
- Walk outside/walk the dog.

- Do yoga or a self-Reiki practice.
- Take a warm bath.
- Do a puzzle (jigsaw, crossword, Words with Friends).
- Watch a funny sitcom or rom-com movie.
- Eat a healthy dinner.
- Make a cup of turmeric and ginger tea with lemon, and take ten long breaths.

What are yours?

Meditation

Try the Happy Place Meditation at donnayferris.com/meditations.

Root Chakra, Color, and Crystal

The root chakra, located at the base of the spine, is the chakra most helpful for this chapter and the next. This chakra is the foundational energy center associated with survival, stability, and grounding. Represented by the color red, the root chakra's key aspects include physical health, security, and connection to the Earth. Crystals such as red jasper, hematite, black tourmaline, and black obsidian are believed to balance this chakra by fostering grounding and stability.

Affirmations

This too shall pass.

I can withstand this.

I will give myself a break today.

It's okay that I need time to grieve.

I can find a little light every day.

Help is a call away (911 or 988).

If I eat, sleep, and exercise, I will feel better.

I can always go to another room or outside to change my energy and how I feel.

I've gotten through difficult times before.

Someday, everything will feel better.

"Almost everything
will work again
if you unplug it for a few
minutes, including you."

Anne Lamott

Chapter Four

Survival of the Nurtured

I woke up and looked at my phone but tried not to pick it up. There was nothing in it I needed – no message that would significantly change my life.

Yet, I couldn't help checking to make sure.

At the same time, I was "exhausterwhelmulated" – exhausted, overwhelmed, and overstimulated all at once.

Can you relate?

Our phones don't help. The next Slack, text, or email message won't alleviate the overwhelm. It'll make it worse.

But before you roll your eyes, I'm not advocating getting rid of phones. I love my phone. Having one handheld device with the ability to connect with others, write, search, listen to podcasts, and take photos has improved my life.

I just need to care about myself enough to use it wisely.

Why Don't We Take Care of Ourselves?

Where else does this impulsive lack of self-care show up in our lives?

Pretty much everywhere, and with good reason.

If you're like me, you too grew up in an environment where taking care of ourselves wasn't a key message. Martyrdom, selflessness, and relentless hard work were the themes of my upbringing.

As a result, it used to take severe illness or profound tragedy for me to fall to my knees and take a break . . . or ask for help.

Meditation teacher, psychologist, and author Tara Brach often says it shouldn't be survival of the fittest but survival of the *nurtured*. To sail easier through difficulty, we need to routinely give ourselves the same care and encouragement we give to those we love.

Think back to a time when you were really happy. Maybe it's when you were getting married, on vacation, or graduating from school. No matter what came, you handled it. You vibrated at a higher energy plane because you were "high" on these astounding events.

This is a state of mind that we can access anytime by filling our "resilience well" with happiness every day. Brené Brown says, "The good news is that joy, collected over time, fuels resilience – ensuring we'll have reservoirs of emotional strength when hard things do happen."

Happiness Starts in Our Morning Routine

How do you start your day? Do you reach for the phone and start doomscrolling, or do you take five, ten, or fifteen minutes for yourself? There are 1,440 minutes in each day – how many do you set aside for yourself?

Social scientist Arthur Brooks says, "Happiness is a combination of enjoyment, satisfaction, and purpose." A daily centering ritual allows us to pause and focus on these three essential tools for loss recovery. It also gives us a break to remember our highest, most divine self, how we feel about our life, and commit our day to our Dharma – what we were put on earth to do (more on that in Chapter Eleven).

Our divinity and purpose are our best guide, and a centering practice helps us get out of our ego trance and return to who we are and want to be. It also reminds us that what we pay attention to is who we are. And if we aren't aware of what we're focusing on, we will fritter our lives away and look back with regret.

Commitment to a morning centering practice was modeled for me in childhood. I watched my parents start their days reading the Daily Guidepost (a book of inspirational words and scripture), followed by a prayer of guidance for their day.

I fell back into the arms of this ritual when my marriage fell apart. Monthly yoga philosophy reading assignments were included in the yoga therapy training I was completing at the time. To get them done, I read a chapter every morning. Soon after Mario died, I added meditating for five to ten minutes and writing my "spinning" thoughts in my journal.

This has expanded into picking an Oracle card (a tool to connect with your intuition) and sometimes a Reiki meditation or yoga practice. But at the core, it begins with devotional reading, meditation, and writing my thoughts, which includes a list of things I want to do that take me closer to who I want to be and what I care about.

For example, my list today included research on an upcoming

trip, editing two chapters of this book, sending a sympathy card to someone who lost her father, and ordering dog food for my beloved Jake, the Wonder Dog.

The practice takes anywhere from ten to twenty minutes, and consistency is key. If I don't make time for this simple ritual, my day is shot. I look back at the end of my worst days and can see how many times I was in a daze – far from what I wanted to accomplish and who I wanted to be.

The timing of this ritual is essential, too. Taking care of yourself first thing in the morning is crucial. If you wait, something else – kids, jobs, chores, etc. – will always get in the way.

Make a Plan

Take five minutes now and plan your ten-to-twenty-minute morning ritual. Write it in your journal pages. Schedule it on your calendar. Then, tell someone else (or email me) the details. When starting a habit, it helps to share it with someone else to commit to it.

Some of my favorite books for my daily centering practice are *Journey to the Heart: Daily Meditations on the Path to Freeing Your Soul* by Melody Beattie, *Meditations for Women Who Do Too Much* by Anne Wilson Schaef, and *The Daily Book of Positive Quotations* by Linda Picone.

In addition to a daily meditation ritual, you can follow other self-care practices. These commitments are more than the emergency self-care discussed in the last chapter. They are routine investments

"There are 1,440 minutes in a day – how many do you set aside for yourself?"

Donna Y. Ferris

in your well-being, which, for me, include:

- Walking my dog, Jake
- Reading/writing
- A cup of hot water with lemon when I get up
- Drinking more water than coffee (or anything else)
- Eating foods and taking supplements that are supportive of mental health (B-complex vitamins, Omega 3s, Lion's Mane, nuts, and dark green leafy vegetables)
- Stretching and meditation before bed
- Listening to my Al Jarreau Pandora playlist and dancing in the shower
- Regular spa visits for massages, facials, and pedicures
- Therapist/life coaching appointments

These healthy routines lift me just enough to resonate higher so I can feel better and see a way out of what I'm going through. Positive psychologist Maria Sirois calls this three percent happier, which feels possible. Trying for anything more seems impossible when we're recovering from loss.

This isn't easy. Hurting ourselves by numbing with unhealthy behaviors might feel instinctive. On the other hand, facing our feelings and persisting through hard times can be a slog, but it's led me to the most amazing journey and community.

Let's get started now. Pull out your journal, and list ten healthy activities that will support your recovery journey. Also, consider including a supportive song, TV show, or movie playlist (suggestions in the back of this book). Take a picture of your healthy self-care list and post it on your phone, or put the list on a sticky note at your desk.

Boundaries

Another essential way to practice self-care is to set boundaries – limits for both your work and personal life.

Setting boundaries is like drawing lines in the sand to show what's acceptable and what's not in our relationships and lives. It's saying, "Hey this is where I stand." Hopefully before issues arise (rather than blowing up afterward).

As a people pleaser, I have trouble with boundaries. I always want to show how I can help but feel taken advantage of when my imaginary lines are crossed. What I try to do now is notice how I feel when doing something for another. Am I light and happy – or is there a flutter of resentment in my chest? Do I find myself stomping, slumping, or slamming things? If so, my body is telling me that all is not as it seems (more on this in Chapter Eight), and it's time to look for a graceful way to communicate my needs. This is a great thing to work through with your therapist or life coach, as there is no pat answer – everything is situational.

That said, creating boundaries has the side benefit of allowing us to create genuine connections with others. We give those close to us the chance to hear our true feelings; as a result, they can get closer to us – and grow by doing more for themselves.

Forgiving and Boundaries

I was always taught to forgive and turn the other cheek. But when I began studying Buddhist philosophy, I learned that not only is forgiving essential but so is refusing to open ourselves to additional harm.

Forgiveness is important because it provides a release of the pain that was caused. It isn't an act but an acceptance. When we genuinely forgive, an issue no longer has power over us. This applies to forgiving ourselves, too.

When forgiving, it also helps to remember that those who hurt us are actually hurting themselves (which is why they exhibit destructive behaviors). And if possible, wish them well. We can use the Metta meditation: "May they be happy, may they be healthy, may they be safe, may they live a life with ease."

Then? Set a firm boundary they can never cross again!

This reminds me of a quote by Maya Angelou: "When someone shows you who they are, believe them the first time." Wise words.

We are Enough

It's important to remember that at our center, we are good, kind, and exactly where we're supposed to be.

We are enough.

We just need to remember that and get out of our own way. And not let those into our lives who do not believe in us or wouldn't choose to support us when we leave the room (more on this in Chapter Nine).

And the more you take care of yourself, set healthy boundaries, and focus on your purpose, the more likely they will find you.

Self-Love is the Foundation

I hope this chapter has provided the foundation for a lifelong self-nurturing practice, a key foundation for handling any challenge we face.

Another essential learning to bounce back stronger is befriending and reframing our thoughts. More on that in the Mind Game chapter – coming up next.

Journaling Exercise

Create a daily centering ritual. Include what you will drink, the type of candle you might light, a book to use for a short reading (or pick one from the resources in the back of this book), and a guided meditation from donnayferris.com/meditations. Add something from your list of healthy self-care activities to fit into your day. Try this every morning (or at least 3-5 days each week) for a month, and note any changes in your journaling pages that occur as a result.

Meditation

Try the Loving Kindness Meditation at donnayferris.com/meditations (or listen to the last fifteen minutes of episode 11 of the *Bounce Back Stronger* podcast with Sharon Salzberg).

Root Chakra, Color and Crystals

The root chakra, located at the base of the spine, is the chakra most helpful for this chapter and the last. This chakra is the foundational energy center associated with survival, stability, and grounding. Represented by the color red, the root chakra's key aspects include physical health, security, and connection to the Earth. Crystals such as red jasper, hematite, black tourmaline, and black obsidian are believed to balance this chakra by fostering grounding and stability.

Affirmations

I am worthy of my own care.

I am a priority in my own life.

I take care of myself as I would someone I love.

I am enough.

I am deserving of contentment, joy, and peace.

I have the right to complete all my needs.

I nourish my body every day.

I believe in my goodness.

I am worthy of infinite and unending compassion.

I look forward to taking care of myself today.

I will look for small ways to show care for myself.

JOURNAL

"The way we experience the world around us is a direct reflection of the world within us."

Gabby Bernstein

Chapter Five

The Mind Game

I was slurping my first coffee in the family room when Mario barreled in. His eyes were wide, and he was talking fast. "We need to get stuff from the Amish Market for the Super Bowl." The big game was the next day.

Hungover and still trying to form sentences, I said, "Wait 'til I finish this, and I'll go with you."

"No. I want to get there when they open to get the wings and bread you like. It'll be a madhouse later."

"Okay, okay. Before you go, can you send me the link to that computer mouse you wanted for Valentine's Day?" He sat and sent me a text with the link. Then, he started talking about some cooking posts on Facebook. I barely listened.

Instead, I read from *The Untethered Soul* by Michael A. Singer, a book that until that morning, had gathered dust on my bookshelf. I highlighted a quote about being so peaceful you could handle anything the day brings.

Mario said something about not wanting to disturb me, and when he kissed the crown of my head, I barely looked up. It was 7:50 a.m. The Amish Market opened at 8:00. I spent the next thirty minutes buying the mouse on Amazon and reading a chapter of

Elizabeth Gilbert's book, *Big Magic,* for a writing group I had to lead that week. I made a meme of one of the quotes, and as I posted it, I heard an ambulance siren.

It seemed to be coming from the Amish Market, a block away. I looked at my watch: 8:40. Mario should be back now. I texted him. No response.

I texted again. Nothing.

I called him. It went to voicemail.

*   *   *

Over the following nine days, I would lean on *The Untethered Soul's* guidance as my life broke apart from Mario's massive stroke and eventual passing.

The book was a lifeline. It still is.

If you don't have a copy, please get one.

Our Mind Under Duress

One of *The Untethered Soul's* primary themes is that everything we think is not necessarily true. Our thoughts are not reality. They are stories we tell ourselves to feel safe, and we can change and reshape them anytime.

This isn't as helpful when first facing heart-wrenching situations because our minds are numb with shock. We can't handle the impact of the blow or the life alterations this new event is making, and we may even short-circuit for a brief time.

Then, when we can, we start to process what has happened and absorb the magnitude of the changes it will cause to our future and who we are.

Our Suffering is in Our Hands

This may sound unbelievable, but how we interpret an event is entirely up to us. We can change how we experience pain and loss by watching the mind spinning instead of getting absorbed in its chatter. A meditation practice aids this process by helping us detach from our thoughts and befriend our minds. This is especially helpful when our brain is agitated by difficulties. That's when the stories worsen.

This knowledge doesn't lessen the impact, though. For example, feelings of loss over Mario's death and guilt over not being present when he had his stroke can surface for me at any time. But when I realize my thoughts are just ruminations, and nothing is harming me now, I can observe them, apply some self-care, and they flow away.

Rethinking Our Problems

Another way to use the mind game is to change our beliefs about difficulties. For example, Mario's illness and eventual death broke me open, which provided an opportunity for me to change for the better. Losing someone precious made me stop taking love and life for granted. Today, I'm more aware and work to cherish every moment with those I love. I try not to let life's struggles (or drinking alcohol) keep me from feeling joy when it comes.

That doesn't mean I don't have periods of pain when I'm angry or sad because work or life has disappointed me somehow. But I bounce back quicker from those periods. And after a time, I can reframe what's happened. I can tell a new story and make a new plan. I identify little ways to lift my heart and build on those better feelings until I can climb out of the emotional hole.

This is what I call the "mind game," and you can play it, too.

Questioning Our Thoughts

In moments of loss and hardship, being curious and questioning our thoughts can be helpful to reframe our perspective. Instead of accepting every thought as an unalterable reality, we can play with them and get curious about their validity, which opens us to the possibility of a different outcome. We can ask ourselves if these thoughts are helping us. Do they advance our healing or keep us stuck in grief? Shifting our mindset helps us move toward the understanding that suffering is an inherent part of life, and it is our attachment to fixed beliefs that intensifies and prolongs our pain.

Sometimes, we try to fit what is happening within our minds into a neat little puzzle. But life isn't like that – and growth occurs when we accept that the pieces may not fit, or some may be missing, and maybe the puzzle was never the point.

Try this now – go to your journaling pages and list the things bothering you. Don't censor them in any way.

Then look at them. Here's an idea that will change your life (and likely piss you off at first).

That list is your teacher.

Each one of those items is something you will learn and grow from. They are issues or people you are resisting – instead of accepting them as they are now. You are in a "thinking prison."

But you can set yourself free.

Ninety Percent of Our Thoughts are the Same

Stanford University Professor Fred Luskin's research states that we have 60,000 thoughts daily, and 90 percent are the same as yesterday's. And more of our brain matter is focused on the negative (things that bother us) rather than the positive of any situation (this is part of our survival mechanisms). But we can change that. We can harness our thoughts and rise above rumination to be in the moment – and find peace by accepting what comes.

There is a phrase in many spiritual texts (and frequently used in benedictions) called "the peace that passes all understanding." No matter what we are presented with, we can observe the situation (not let our mind ruminate about the past or fly into the future) and realize we are safe in this moment. It doesn't mean we aren't affected by what's happening. But we don't have to give up our ability to find moments of peace. (The meditation at the end of this chapter is a great way to practice this skill).

"Sometimes, we try to fit what is happening within our minds into a neat little puzzle. But life isn't like that – and growth occurs when we accept that the pieces may not fit, or some may be missing, and maybe the puzzle was never the point."

Donna Y. Ferris

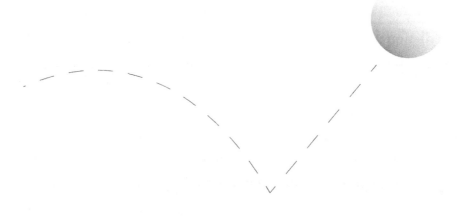

Once we develop this ability to find peace, we can start to look at what is bothering us differently. Where might we *accept* what is happening? We don't have to stay in situations that are bothering us or with people who are detrimental to our mental health. We have to accept that we cannot change them and move on.

Bottom line? Our response to life and our happiness are entirely in our control. Or as Ralph Waldo Emerson said, "Nobody can bring you peace but yourself."

The Resilient Persona

What if we build on the persona idea introduced in Chapter Three and take on the persona of a person who recovers no matter what?

Taking on personas can be very helpful in making changes. When we start exercising more frequently or eating healthier, we take on a fit person persona. This can help us stay the course and reinforce the habits we are trying to instill. Similarly, if we take on the habits and thinking of a resilient person, we may find ourselves more assured in moving forward through this difficult time.

One of my favorite examples of taking on a persona is from the hit TV show *Ally McBeal*[1]. Lawyer John Cage uses Barry White's songs to give himself confidence in the courtroom (and in the bedroom).

How might you take on a resilient persona? Is there an affirmation or song that might support you? Mine is Journey's

"Don't Stop Believin'." Every time it comes on, I'm comforted and reassured with all of life's possibilities.

With this initial understanding of how to harness the mind (supported by reading *The Untethered Soul*), we can begin to process our feelings (we will work on this in the next chapter).

Journaling Exercise

List the items that are bothering you. Where can you accept what is happening and take the best action for yourself rather than waiting for something or someone to change? Where have you done this in the past? What did you learn as a result? How did you take care of yourself during that time? What skills did you gain? How has your life changed or improved? What words would you use to describe yourself in relation to this situation? How might you reshape that loss story and apply what you learned to what you're going through now? How can you use this new story to shape your resilient persona?

Meditation

Try the Peace that Passes All Understanding Meditation at donnayferris.com/meditations.

Third Eye Chakra, Color, and Crystal

The third eye chakra is the sixth energy center in the traditional chakra system. It is positioned at the forehead, slightly above the space between the eyebrows. Associated with intuition, perception, and spiritual insight, the third eye chakra is linked to the color indigo or deep blue. This chakra fosters inner wisdom and the ability to see beyond the physical realm. Crystals such as amethyst, lapis lazuli, and fluorite are commonly used to balance the third eye chakra.

Affirmations

I am not my thoughts.
I am a resilient person.
I trust the timing of my life.
I take every moment one at a time.
I am grateful for the present moment.
I can find peace in this moment.
What is meant for me will not pass me.
I am the architect of my happiness and can choose it every day.
Every day is a chance to create a life I love.
I can bounce back stronger from this.

"Every storm
runs out of rain."

Maya Angelou

Chapter Six

Feelings Inside, Not Expressed

It was 9:30 p.m. on a Thursday. One hand was deep inside a Cheddar Jack Cheez-It box, and the other held a full wine glass. An empty bottle of Chardonnay rested on the side table, and *Million Dollar Listing Los Angeles* was on TV.

When I came to at 3:00 a.m., I was bloated and anxious, and the first thing I thought was: "*Why can't I stop doing this?*"

Because I was so exhausted from keeping the wheels turning on the work and mommy "bus" that the stuffed feelings of frustration, fear, and anger erupted. Not knowing any better, I numbed the uncomfortable energy with junk food, reality TV, and wine.

This would still be my Thursday night routine if I hadn't started tracking my food and wine intake. That's when I recognized it as an unhealthy habit.

Why can't we let our feelings out instead of bottling them up?

Because at some point, we learned it wasn't okay to feel or express our feelings or that it was dangerous to do so. Maybe because they threatened or embarrassed others.

At age four, my parents forced me to sit through church services. As an ordinarily active four-year-old, I didn't take well to this. I would sing, crawl under the pews, or cry at the sad Bible stories, ending with my mother pulling me into the church basement and beating me while simultaneously shushing my cries. Eventually, I connected getting hit with being myself. In response, I shut down my emotions and a lot of who I was. I tried to be the "good girl" to avoid abuse.

Where did you learn how to handle your feelings? How are those teachings affecting your career, life, work, and relationships today? Write what comes to mind about this topic in your journaling pages.

Then ask yourself how you might embrace the emotions and express them safely? We can start by using them as a clue instead of stuffing them down. One of my clues is saying, "I'm fine." Whenever I utter it, I know I'm hiding my feelings.

What does "fine" even mean? The definition of the word is "very well." But is that what we say when things are going very well? No, we say that everything's "excellent," "amazing," or "wonderful." We don't say "fine." (A perfect example of this can be found in Prince William's repeated use of the word in Episode Six of the last season of the Netflix series *The Crown*.)

Maybe a more appropriate definition of the word is "Feelings Inside, Not Expressed."

Our Bodies Can't Hide Our Feelings

What other clues appear when unexpressed feelings are present? Watch a video call or an in-person group discussion live or on TV.

Do you see people doing any of the following:
- Covering their mouth when another is talking.
- Scratching the back of their head.
- Taking a drink when they're asked a difficult question or disagree with the speaker.
- Interrupting when an uncomfortable piece of information is expressed.
- Shaking their knees, hands, or feet.

These are clues to unexpressed feelings. Others that may show up in us:
- Sudden all-over warmth
- A desire for salty or sweet food
- The *need* to drink alcohol or take drugs
- An urge to go shopping or gamble.
- Picking at scabs or cutting.

These are signs we're trying to ignore or avoid a feeling. When these behaviors are present, we can use them as hints to *allow* our emotions to be felt and safely expressed – even ones as intense as anger (a relative of fear or sadness). When angry, it may be helpful to ask what you fear. How do you feel threatened? Are you sad about something? How can you feel safe enough to harness these feelings into something helpful?

Keeping emotions inside is harmful not only to our health (it can cause increased blood pressure, ulcers and other digestion complications, muscle pain, anxiety, and depression) but also to our relationships.

People can tell when we're upset. We give off an energy that's undeniable. In the Oscar-nominated movie, *A Man Called Otto*, the title character is grieving the death of his wife but isn't managing his feelings. He's stuck in grief and grumpy and challenging as a result. His tone is sharp, his words short, and his facial expressions are dark and wrinkled. He is rude to one woman, but she sees he's hurting and puts her foot in the way when he tries to close the door on her. She won't turn away, and that's where his healing begins.

Unspoken feelings can put people off and derail us at work or home. We don't express our feelings because we're afraid we'll get into trouble like we did as a child or our feelings will overwhelm us. But not expressing them can lead to the same outcome, with the addition of possibly getting fired, facing a divorce, or becoming ill.

Don't Lean Into the Drama

What can we do instead? We can give ourselves a break. There is no morality in feelings, only in behavior. We can feel angry without hurting anyone – and once we feel the feelings, apply some self-care (like a walk outside or sipping a cup of chamomile tea) and let them ebb and eventually flow away. While it may seem counterintuitive, the pain is better felt than resisted.

These emotionally charged times are like being on the razor's edge – the brink between normalcy and chaos. We see and feel things clearly and viscerally. Our ability to express ourselves gracefully or guardedly is lowered.

When we are raw like this, I say, *don't lean into the drama.* Sometimes, past trauma and conditioning can make intense situations feel familiar and comfortable. But engaging with negative energy can cause a figurative (or actual) hangover and disrupt our healing.

Recently, I attended an outdoor concert. I looked forward to it all week. It had the perfect elements. The weather was cool and breezy, the band was upbeat, the panini was delicious, and a spontaneous dancing love train broke out.

But in the middle of the event, someone made an offhand comment. It had to do with my appearance (my weight). I'm sure it wasn't meant to sting, but it certainly did.

A book reviewer of my memoir complained that I didn't go far enough into my weight battle, saying that I glided on the edge of it but didn't share that pain. And she was right. Those pages fell onto the cutting room floor (and it may be the subject of a future book). There was so much else to fit into those 299 pages that my tango with my 200+-pound girth felt superfluous.

I'm not going to go into it here beyond the fact that I'm healthier now than I've been in years, mainly because I've finally befriended my body (more on that in Chapter Eight) and gotten off the sugar rollercoaster by becoming sober. That said, I will likely always be a large or double-digit size, and I'm usually okay with that.

So, let's get back to the comment at the concert.

When the words landed, my eyes widened, and my face grew warm. I looked around to see if anyone else heard, but they were caught up in other conversations. And as happens with people who are clumsy with their words, the commenter was on to a new subject before I could say anything.

So I remained silent. Nothing I said was going to change

anything. Eventually, the band launched into a familiar song, and the commenter danced away.

Since I noticed my uncomfortable feelings, I didn't do what I sometimes do – binge on sugary or salty snacks (or drink away my upset). Instead, I watched some *Real Housewives* episodes (living vicariously from their witty retorts) and meditated with Reiki (to release the energy) before bed. I woke up hangover-free, which gave me the time and wakefulness to work on my writing.

The takeaway? When you're going through dukkha (the Pali word for suffering), and someone throws more at you . . . duck! Don't make everything worse by responding in kind or letting it sabotage your self-care. We always regret it afterward, even though the incident probably won't matter much in a week, month, or year.

We Cannot Change People

The second insight to remember when emotions are intense is that we can't change people. They have their worries and fears, and they will behave and speak based on them. We can only control our own actions or inaction.

Sometimes, we attract challenging people. They show up as bosses we hate, partners we divorce, and friends we ghost. If we grow up with neurotic or narcissistic parents, similar people will initially feel like home. The only way to break away from that pattern is to love ourselves enough to see these people for who they are.

"When you're going through dukkha (the Pali word for suffering), and someone throws more at you . . . duck! Don't make everything worse by responding in kind or letting it sabotage your self-care. We always regret it afterward, even though the incident probably won't matter much in a week, month, or year."

Donna Y. Ferris

Then, we can:

- **WALK AWAY FROM A SITUATION THAT'S TOO INTENSE –** You can always say you must go to the bathroom or have to answer the door, or if you're on a call, say the connection is terrible. Sometimes, just cutting off the conversation for a few minutes is enough to let the feelings dissipate, making it easier to address them.

- **SET BOUNDARIES –** When I first got divorced, people asked me inappropriate questions about the settlement, how I felt about my ex-husband, or who I was dating. I learned over time to say, "That isn't a question I'm going to answer."

- **MEDITATE TO LET THE FEELINGS OF PAIN WASH OVER YOUR BODY** – Allow the pain to sink down into the earth (the rose meditation practice accompanying this chapter is excellent for this) or along an imaginary river in your mind's eye.

Some other ways to navigate your feelings include:

- **JOURNAL,** and if acceptable, share your feelings constructively.

- **ENGAGE IN ENERGY-RELEASING ACTIVITIES,** such as yoga, singing, dancing, or painting.

- **GIVE YOURSELF TIME TO SIT WITH YOUR FEELINGS AND NOTICE HOW THEY EBB.** No feeling lasts forever.

- **TALK ABOUT YOUR FEELINGS WITH A THERAPIST,** life coach, or trusted friend.

- **REFRAME YOUR SELF-TALK,** as described in the previous chapter.

Yet. . .

That brings me to a third insight that involves one of my favorite words – Yet.

Sometimes, when going through difficult times, we catastrophize our feelings. We think, "I will never be happy," or "I can't find love," "Career success is not for me," or "My kids aren't settled and happy."

Find a way to add the word "yet" to those sentences. Hope is the key to survival. You have to keep the door open just a bit to the possibility that it will all work out . . . and then, chances are it will.

And as soon as possible, try to stop wallowing, take good care of yourself, and return to generating positive vibrations. Adopt that resilient persona we talked about in the last chapter. Did you know faking a smile gives your body the same feelings as a real one? Giving yourself even a manufactured boost of positivity can lift your spirits.

St. Elmo's Fire

What is the final thing to remember when navigating "the feels"? Don't get distracted by something else to avoid facing your feelings and problems. In the movie *St. Elmo's Fire*, there is a scene where the character, played by Demi Moore, focuses on planning her stepmother's funeral (she's still alive) rather than the issues in her life that are blowing up.

The character played by Rob Lowe (a longtime sober warrior in real life) tells her she's focusing on this ridiculous thing because her other issues are too big. This avoidance was making a mess of her life.

That's what we do. But we can choose a different way. We can look at life as it is now and feel the feelings instead of resisting, numbing, or distracting ourselves from them. We can take good care of ourselves while this happens. Then, the feelings have the opportunity to dissipate.

It isn't easy, so the next chapter is devoted to overcoming one of my frequent foes: resistance.

Journaling Exercise

How can you give yourself a timeout when faced with "big" feelings? What ways have worked in the past? Maybe write these ways down on a sticky note, along with the Maya Angelou quote from the beginning of the chapter or another one that inspires you to let the feelings be and dissipate.

Meditation

Try the Rose Meditation at donnayferris.com/meditations.

Heart Chakra, Color and Crystals

The heart chakra may be helpful for this chapter. This chakra is the fourth energy center at the chest's center. It is associated with the color green or pink, and it governs emotions, compassion, love, and connection. It acts as a bridge between the lower and upper chakras, balancing an individual's physical and spiritual characteristics. Crystals and gems like rose quartz, green aventurine, and emerald are commonly used to open and balance the heart chakra.

Affirmations

It is safe to feel.

It's okay to walk away from situations that make me uncomfortable.

I don't have to let situations disturb me.

No feeling lasts forever.

I let go of my pain.

What I want is on the way.

When I let go of resentment, I make room for love.

I'm growing stronger and more assured with every breath I take.

I trust the Universe/God and their plan for me.

#Feelittohealit

JOURNAL

"The boundary to
what we can accept is
the boundary
to our freedom."

Tara Brach

Chapter Seven

Resistance is Futile

I poured the huge bottle of Miralax into a pitcher of orange Gatorade. I can't remember the last time I willingly drank this syrupy sweet liquid.

Maybe never.

It took me ten minutes to choke down half.

"You might want to park yourself next to the bathroom," my husband said.

I nodded and ignored, continuing to putter around the house doing laundry, taking the dog out, and checking work emails.

"This isn't so bad," I said to myself. "Why does everyone complain about colonoscopy prep?"

Hours later, soiled clothes were draped all over the bathroom, and I was stationed on our bed, ready to run to the toilet quickly.

It would have been much easier if I'd only accepted what was happening to me.

But that isn't how we're wired.

Let It Go

When my youngest daughter is home from college one of our favorite things to do together is watch *Star Trek: The Next Generation* episodes. Our favorite nemesis is the Borg. Their catchphrase? *Resistance is futile.*

Just typing it makes me shiver.

But it's true. Resistance prevents us from adjusting to what's happening. It traps us in our worst moments, leaving us to relive them over and over.

It also generates a feeling of helplessness that lingers in our minds and bodies. When faced with similar situations or memories of the original event, we are triggered and fall into a trance of fear, overreaction, and depression.

Want to get out of this cycle? Let it go.

Stop resisting.

One way to do that is to feel the feelings, write them out, and let them wash over your body. If the event is particularly traumatic or challenging to release, seek therapy, grief groups, and/or holistic support (Reiki, EFT, EMDR, acupuncture, etc.). But whatever you do, move through the feelings.

Getting stuck in resistance will make you feel like a victim.

I've been there. I've had my life dangling at the end of the thinnest piece of yarn over a chasm, echoing like the Grand Canyon. After multiple difficulties, I believed it was spinning perfectly clockwise, but somehow, it reversed motion and began to career out of control.

Eventually, I caught my breath, stopped saying, "I'm fine," and let all the emotions sink into and over me. I asked for help and eventually accepted that difficult things happen, even if we meditate daily, hydrate, do the tree pose, and own enough crystals to balance the chakras of every single person at Disney World on Presidents' Day.

Of Course. . .

If you're lucky, the people who've helped you and heard every miserable, messy, musty emotion will say something that changes everything: "Of course, you feel that way."

Of course.

Two of the most beautiful words in the English language.

They let us off the hook and provide space to accept what's happening rather than resist. Those words take us from the cesspool of victimhood to the land of victory. They unlock the door to profound healing.

Because, of course, suffering is an inherent part of human existence.

The Mustard Seed

One of my favorite stories about the Buddha involves a woman who comes to him carrying her dead son. Understandably, she's devastated and begs the Buddha to bring her son back to life. After he listens and calms her, he asks her to go to all the houses in the village and obtain a mustard seed from each home that hadn't suffered loss. When she does this, he will bring her son back to life.

Does she come back with any seeds?

No. Every house she visits has also experienced loss. She returns to the Buddha with this knowledge – and the acceptance and willingness to heal.

When we accept that suffering is a given – something everyone faces – we can begin to look for ways to integrate the experiences and learn from them.

We may even begin to see these trials as gifts.

Can you look back and see such events in your life? Times when you were sure you would never survive? Turning points that changed everything for the better? That led you to a new way of being or the strength to try something you've always wanted to do?

Write them down. Keep them as reminders that you've overcome difficult times and are better for it.

Life Happens *For* Us

We aren't victims of our lives. Life happens *for* us.

We rarely evolve when life is good. Typically, it takes a painful loss to examine our existence and seek ways to improve it. Why? Because it's then we realize how little time we have.

If there's pain, there's a lesson. Something is working through us. And once the energy dissipates, calm, wisdom, and purpose follow.

Our body can provide helpful clues to speed the path to healing. More on that in the next chapter.

Journaling Exercise

Write about something you are resisting. How does it feel? What would giving into it feel like? Try allowing the situation to

"We aren't
victims of our lives.
Life happens
for us."

Donna Y. Ferris

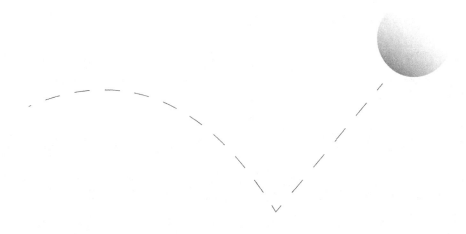

be. Try to accept it. What are you holding onto? What does it feel like to let it go? Is there anything positive about letting it go? If this is too difficult for you to do alone, talk to your therapist, life coach, or grief counselor.

Also, how is your plant doing? Take a moment to document its growth (maybe draw it, or measure how high it is). Share its progress with friends and family or on social media. If it didn't grow for some reason, there are always more seeds, so try again (or decide this is not for you, and that's okay).

Meditation

Try the Overcoming Resistance Meditation at donnayferris.com/meditations.

Solar Plexus Chakra, Color and Crystals

The solar plexus chakra may be helpful for this and the next chapter. This chakra is the third energy center located in the upper abdomen, near the diaphragm. Represented by the color yellow, this chakra is associated with personal power, self-confidence, and the transformative energy of the sun. This chakra also governs one's sense of identity and willpower. Crystals such as citrine, yellow tiger's eye, and amber are often utilized to balance and activate this chakra.

Affirmations

What I resist persists.

I am powerful.

Life happens for us.

I release resistance to _____.

I am strong enough to overcome any obstacle.

I allow this to be.

My mind is open to creative solutions and opportunities.

I know I can handle any challenge I face.

The moment I release resistance is the moment I'm mentally free.

I'm letting the Universe/God figure it out.

"And I said
to my body softly,
'I want to be your friend.'
It took a long breath and
replied, 'I've been waiting
my whole life for this.'"

Nayyirah Waheed

Chapter Eight

Body Wisdom

I have no idea how he found me – and I'm a bit peeved to be standing behind a salon reception desk, receiver in hand. This would be marginally acceptable, but I look like a satellite with crinkled aluminum foil pieces all over my head. Not to mention the lobby is full of people gawking as I try to calm the whining male on the other end of the line.

"I know it's Sunday, Donna, but you've got to come in. I can't figure this asset-liability spreadsheet out without you. And the bastards want the report on Wednesday."

Yeah, I know. That's why I asked you to review it two weeks ago. "Can't this wait till tomorrow morning? I'll be there first thing." I sink into the receptionist's chair and grab a handful of peanut M&M's from the counter candy jar.

"I have an 8:00 a.m. tee time tomorrow with the city pension manager. It's going to be 50 degrees. Not many more golf days with winter coming."

The irony. He wants *me* to come in on Sunday because *he'll* be golfing during regular business hours. Although he'll say he's working. But does anyone believe that golfing with clients is work?

"I'm kinda in the middle of something," I whisper – no need to give the lobby participants more entertainment than necessary.

"You keep saying you want to be promoted and have your own team. This is how you get there, darlin' – by making things happen."

Darlin'? For God's sake, he was born in Allegheny County, PA. "Okay. Okay. I'll be there in an hour."

"Make it 30 minutes – I know where that salon is, and it's only 15 minutes away with Sunday traffic."

* * *

I'm repeatedly attracted to people like this. At first, they seem funny and intelligent. They charm every room they walk into, and I'm honored when they confide their dissatisfaction with someone else's performance.

But once inside their circle, my blinders come off. I see them snapping for no reason and putting everyone on edge with conflicting praise and fiercely negative feedback. I realize their "caring" actions aren't altruistic – they're conspiring to get what they want.

Their behavior puts me in a tizzy. I feel hurt because they obviously don't care about me or anyone else. In response, I eat unhealthy food, can't sleep at night, and every part of my being is knotted and tense.

Body Wisdom

My body knows that the person is like my mother. Once my brain catches up, the wrinkles on my forehead soften, my shoulders drop, and I breathe easier.

I'm attracted to this type of person because they feel familiar. As a result, my subconscious mind tries to figure out how to make them love me. "This time, I can do it," I think. "Everything will work out if I anticipate their every whim, execute it flawlessly, and make them look good. Right?"

Nope.

People like this don't value loyalty or caring. I've spent years (decades even) seeking approval from these archetypes because I never got it from my mother. I leave (or get pushed from) these relationships, feeling shame, guilt, and self-loathing each time . . . all because I got duped again.

Psychologist Alice Miller sums up the phenomenon, "The truth about our childhood is stored up in our body, and although we can repress it, we can never alter it. Our intellect can be deceived, our feelings manipulated, and conceptions confused…But someday, our body will present the bill."

For me, the bill shows up in extra pounds.

I doubt I'll ever stop being attracted to these people, but now I notice my body's reactions to them faster. Its wisdom saves me.

Pema Always Knows

I could rage against the universe, but somehow, it always brings me the life lesson I need. Like Pema Chödrön says, "Nothing ever goes away until it has taught us what we need to know." Learning how to deal with people like my mother healthily is a lifelong lesson for me.

One of my favorite scenes from the Oscar-winning movie *Good Will Hunting* is when Robin Williams's psychotherapist character repeatedly tells Will Hunting (played by Matt Damon) that his childhood abuse is not his fault.

Will rejects all the love and good fortune he's offered because he believes he doesn't deserve it. He's internalized all the abuse and pain he suffered as a child because he believes he *did* deserve that.

This can happen to us too. We might grow up feeling we did something wrong that justifies the mistreatment received, but that isn't true. If we don't realize this, we continue to be attracted to the wrong people and reject healthy ones. (If you relate to this, please consider sharing this realization with your therapist.) It's helpful for anyone suffering from childhood wounds to reframe their feelings like Williams' character did with Damon's.

The biggest clue for me that a person is triggering my maternal past is my sympathetic nervous system becomes charged. This body structure focuses on responding to dangerous or stressful situations, even when perfectly safe. So when I'm with them – even in a harmless conference room – I find myself short of breath, queasy, and visibly jittery.

The Benefits of Yoga

Soon after identifying my latest triggering person (there is always one around, it seems), my husband said after one of my lengthy rants, "Hey, have you been doing yoga lately?"

I'd been teaching regular yoga classes online since the pandemic but recently stopped because the pace at work had quickened. Could that have lowered my ability to see and cope with this situation?

As the book, *The Body Keeps the Score: Brain, Mind, and Body in the Healing of Trauma*, by Bessel van der Kolk, M.D. says, yoga's breathing and movement practices provide a release helpful in calming the sympathetic nervous system. This allows us to better regulate between the sympathetic (fight or flight) and parasympathetic (rest and digest) nervous systems.

In other words, connecting with our body and breath through yoga allows us to slow down and notice what's happening inside us.

How Do You Feel?

One of my most profound early yoga class experiences was when a teacher asked us how we felt at the start of class. I had never thought to ask myself that. And at the time, I had no way to answer.

It was a simple question, but it can be hard to respond when you aren't connected to your body or understand how past trauma is being triggered in the present. This can lead to impulsive or hysterical responses to current situations – that harm relationships and careers.

In other words, hysterical reactions may be due to historical triggers.

One of my favorite quotes is by Viktor Frankl (more about him

"We are instinctual beings living primarily surface lives."

Donna Y. Ferris

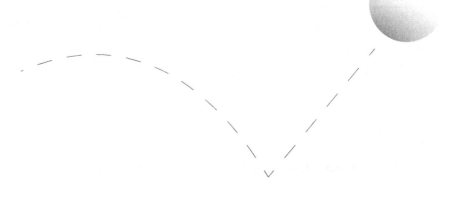

later): "Between stimulus and response, there is a space. And in that space is our freedom."

How do we find that space and the ability to pause? Yoga (as well as Tai Chi, Reiki meditation, EMDR, and EFT) can downregulate our nervous system so we can think more clearly. And since trauma sits in the body, physical practices that involve breathing and movement can heal and release it.

These practices also allow us to stress the body in a healthy way – so we can *practice* resilience. In fact, studies[12] have found that even ten weeks of yoga can reduce trauma-related symptoms.

We Need to Listen to Our Body

For a long time, I tried to therapize, spiritualize, or meditate my way out of my childhood triggers. However, therapy, meditation, and spiritual enlightenment are insufficient when our *body* is actively reliving trauma and grief. We are instinctual beings, living primarily surface lives. It's easy to become disconnected from the profound impact of events and people on our physical being. And when triggered, it can feel like our very lives are threatened even though the "perpetrator" could be thousands of miles away.

When I started taking yoga teacher training, it is unsurprising that I began to discuss my childhood abuse openly, eventually writing about it and finding a community of others who struggled with similar histories.

But getting to a place of loving my body would take much longer.

Hiding the Butt

One summer, between college semesters, I worked at a local diner in Washington, PA. I vividly remember the day when a customer said, "Boy, I'm glad I don't have a butt like yours." This was before Jennifer Lopez came on the scene and made that feature a desirable trait.

I've hidden my posterior in almost every situation since and took every fitness class and performed every physical movement (lunges anyone?) focused on reducing the size of my rear end.

Recently, my mother's house was sold, and thousands of her pictures were sorted and distributed to us. As I spread my stack of photos on the couch, my body struggles were fully displayed. When I was over 230 pounds, trapped in an unhappy marriage, and at 145 pounds, exercising three to four hours a day to stay thin.

I lived and died by the pounds on the scale.

Later, in yoga teacher training, my biggest worry wasn't that I would forget the postures. It was having to turn my back on the class to reveal my deepest insecurity.

But years of yoga practice also helped me connect to my body and learn to love it no matter its shape.

Now, I don't weigh myself, but notice how clothes fit and adjust accordingly. I also take stock every morning of how I feel, and if I'm bloated or tired, I look back on what and when I ate and make changes as needed. This practice eventually made me choose to be sober.

In this process, I've learned to love the body I have. I still struggle with loving it thoroughly, especially as it ages, but my relationship with it is better than ever.

Three Important Questions

When things get tough, we feel overwhelmed, or when we're about to react to something that sets us off, it can help to ask ourselves three simple questions:

- What am I thinking?
- How am I feeling?
- What am I doing?

By taking a moment to think about these questions, we give ourselves a chance to hit the pause button and act in a way that's true to ourselves instead of reacting without thinking.

Having supportive friends, family, and guides who understand and embody this approach has been really important for me in getting through tough times. I'll discuss this more in the next chapter.

Journaling Exercise

Listen to the "How do you feel meditation," and write down what comes to mind. List one thing going forward that you will do to better manage the stress that manifests in your body. Maybe try the twenty-minute yoga practice on my YouTube channel. The link can be found at donnayferris.com/meditations.

Meditation

Try the How Do You Feel Meditation (you will need a tennis ball). Also, consider trying the twenty-minute yoga class at the link on the donnayferris.com/meditations page.

Solar Plexus Chakra, Color and Crystals

The solar plexus chakra is helpful for this chapter and the last. This chakra is the third energy center located in the upper abdomen, near the diaphragm. Represented by the color yellow, this chakra is associated with personal power, self-confidence, and the transformative energy of the sun. This chakra also governs one's sense of identity and willpower. Crystals such as citrine, yellow tiger's eye, and amber are often utilized to balance and activate this chakra.

Affirmations

My body is enough the way it is.

I can listen to my body's signals.

My body hears everything I think, so I must speak kindly.

I trust my body's wisdom.

I give my body the respect it deserves.

My body is a blessing.

I listen to my body's needs.

My mind is a friend to my body.

I choose food that nourishes every cell in my body.

My body can do awesome things.

"We are not meant to live
in isolation…The richness of
life is found in community,
in cooperation, in becoming
part of a greater whole.
Expand your bubble,
drop your shield. Invite love in.
Do not attempt to do it alone."

Jeanette LeBlanc

Chapter Nine

Expand Your Bubble

A last-minute ride request led me to Locust Avenue that Sunday. With all the recent buzz on social media and in the press about this neighborhood, I couldn't help but feel anxious during our drive to Philly.

Were we walking into a combat zone?

What I found buoyed me in a way I cannot explain. We were too late for the Philly Pride Parade, but the surrounding celebration was in full swing. My daughter hugged me goodbye and was quickly lost in the crowd. I gave her a few minutes lead time and then pushed into the fray.

I looked down to see pink and light blue stripes on the street and up to see a group of shirtless people singing and dancing on a large outdoor stage. Soon, I was bopping shoulder-to-shoulder through the colorful crowd.

There wasn't a protester in sight. The celebrators were freely walking and dancing as they smiled ear to ear. There's no greater gift than to express ourselves and be accepted for exactly who we are.

Do you have a place like that?

"We're Wired for Connection"

Brené Brown says, "We're wired for connection. It's in our biology. From birth, we need connection to thrive emotionally, physically, spiritually, and intellectually." As mentioned in Chapter Three, in prehistoric times, we could die if we were separated from the herd. As a result, connecting with others can feel as instinctive and essential to the body as breathing.

When we've experienced loss, engaging with people who've been through similar experiences is crucial. They teach us how to navigate our challenges and help us see that overcoming them is possible.

Places to find connection with others around grief or loss may include:

- Grief groups
- Online/Facebook support groups
- Religious or spiritual communities
- Twelve-step or addiction-related meetings
- Hospice organizations
- Therapy centers
- Online counseling
- Corporate employee resource groups
- Community centers

It's also essential when going through difficulties to be vulnerable in our closest relationships – because no one can read your mind. Be sure to let those who love and care about you know how you feel – and be honest about what you need. Give them the chance to be there for you like you've been there for them. It's an opportunity for them to grow and for your relationship to deepen.

Loneliness is an Epidemic

In mid-2023 Surgeon General Dr. Vivek Murthy stated there is an epidemic of loneliness and isolation in the United States. Even before the pandemic, approximately half of all U.S. adults reported experiencing measurable levels of loneliness.

But we don't want to let just anyone into our lives.

There's a saying that we are the average of the five people we spend the most time with. If that's true, we should intentionally choose who we allow into our daily lives.

With that in mind, it's beneficial to connect with individuals who share similar values and interests. Here are some other groups to consider participating in or places to go for connection:

- Interest groups
- Yoga studios
- Volunteer organizations
- Groups specific to age, gender, sexual preference, or ethnicity
- Religious organizations
- Sports groups
- Book clubs
- Art studios
- Travel groups
- Professional groups
- Podcast-related groups
- Employer-sponsored inclusion groups (if your company doesn't have one, start one)

"There's a saying that we are the average of the five people we spend the most time with. If that's true, we should intentionally choose who we allow into our daily lives."

Donna Y. Ferris

We are not alone

Finally, it's important to remember we are always surrounded by the love of our angels, guides, deities, and loved ones who've passed. Therefore, we are never truly alone.

It's probably important to share a little background here. First, I believe in God and the afterlife – which is why I believe in angels and spirit guides. Remember, I'm a skeptic, but I've first-hand knowledge as I saw the spirit of my Mario ascend as he passed, and I have had many communications from him and others I've lost – as well as other spiritual guides.

It would be easier, maybe, not to share these experiences and knowledge with you – and if this idea bothers you, please skip the rest of this chapter.

But I feel compelled to impart this information as I've found it so comforting to know our spiritual energy continues, even after our last earthly breath. And knowing that our loved ones aren't really gone and their love never dies has been a crucial part of my healing journey.

Since publishing my memoir, I've fielded many questions about spiritual guides and led workshops on connecting with them. This may seem woo-woo to you at first, but I can say unequivocally that it helps our healing to believe in the magic of our connection with lost loved ones, spirit guides, deities, and angels. As a result, the rest of this chapter will focus on the lesser-known group within this list – spiritual guides.

Spiritual Guides

What are spiritual guides? They are ascended beings sent to

help us be our best selves. These guides may include ancestors, lost loved ones, spiritual masters, light beings, animal spirits, universal energy, or our divine higher selves. We may call guides by another name – intuition, which I like to think of as falling into the wisdom and experience of the universe.

Roles spiritual guides play in our lives include the following:

- **PROTECT** us from negativity or anxious thoughts.

- **INCREASE** creativity.

- **GUIDE** us to our life purpose.

- **HELP** us with tough decisions or situations.

- **BRING** the right people into our lives.

- **SEND** clues to remove us from people or situations.

They are most likely to help if we call on them, and we need to be at our highest resonance to hear their guidance. How do we peel away the lower-resonating energies, including fear, anger, sadness, anxiety, guilt, and shame:

- **CREATE** a quiet, sacred space for meditation communication.

- **CLEAR** the mind and cultivate openness.

- **FIND** gratitude for everyday things.

- **SURROUND** ourselves with others on the path.

- **BE AWARE** of and manage our energy and thoughts through meditation, Reiki, yoga, and other practices.

How Do Our Guides Speak to Us?

I was recently part of another corporate reorganization involving giving up some of my old duties and taking on a newer role. Even though I was happy to let go of the old, I felt resentful and resistant.

Before bed one night, I surrendered the situation to my spirit guides. That evening, I dreamed about a childhood event when my mother sold some of my toys at a church flea market. This memory was uncomfortable because I didn't find out about the toys being sold until someone had already purchased them and was leaving with them.

When I viewed the scene in the dream, the toys were of no interest to me anymore. Now that I have a basement full of forgotten possessions of my kids, I can understand my mother's actions. Yes, she should have consulted me about selling the toys, but I wasn't playing with them anymore (just like I didn't want the old job responsibilities).

The guides gave me a dream that transformed my feelings about the job change and let me understand the actions of the decision-makers. This experience gave me the strength to bounce back quickly and move on.

Other ways spiritual guides can connect with us include:
- Prayers
- Messages in songs, TV shows, and photos
- Symbols
- Other people's comments or actions
- Thoughts
- Technological glitches
- Animals
- Sudden opportunities
- Journaling our questions and receiving answers
- Oracle cards – These decks can be a great way to connect with our divine guides. You can pick the decks up at a local spiritual energy store or on Amazon. Just choose the one that calls to you and they come with detailed instructions.

Positive Guidance Only

It's important to note that our guides never offer harmful guidance. If you're having destructive thoughts, you may have encountered a ghost. Ignore them and ask them to leave your presence immediately. Also, don't let polarizing forces, energies, or social media get in the way of your best self, connecting with others, or keeping you from resonating high enough to hear your angels, deities, and loved ones.

One way to keep resonating higher during periods of loss is to focus on happier memories of your lost loved ones. We'll discuss this in the next chapter.

Journaling Exercise

Look for evidence of your guides and angels. Sit in meditation or prayer and speak with them, or write down questions and then start writing answers. See what happens. Be curious – are the answers similar to your usual thoughts – or inspired by a higher power? You can also get an Oracle card deck online or in a book or crystal store and start to work with it. Pull a card daily, write down the guidance that speaks to you, and see what happens.

Meditation

Try the Connecting With Your Spirit Guide Meditation on the donnayferris.com/meditations page.

Chakras, Colors, and Crystals

The majority of the topics in this chapter relate to the Heart Chakra, and the spiritual guide discussion relates to the Crown Chakra.

The heart chakra is the fourth energy center at the chest's center. It is associated with the color green or pink, and it governs emotions, compassion, love, and connection. It acts as a bridge between the lower and upper chakras, balancing an individual's physical and spiritual characteristics. Crystals and gems like rose quartz, green aventurine, and emerald are commonly used to open and balance the heart chakra.

The crown chakra is the seventh and highest energy center and is located at the top of the head. Symbolized by the color violet or white, this chakra represents spiritual connection, divine consciousness, and enlightenment. It serves as the gateway to higher states of awareness and understanding. Crystals such as amethyst, clear quartz, and selenite are often used to balance and activate the crown chakra.

Affirmations

I am not alone.

I have a support system that surrounds and supports me.

If I resonate higher, I will access my guides.

I will find others on my path.

I am surrounded by love and light.

I see the world as a kind, loving, and beautiful place.

I trust that the Universe/God gives me exactly what I need at exactly the right time.

I am divinely protected, inspired, and guided by the Universe/God.

Everything is unfolding in perfect timing.

I have unshakable faith in my divine path.

"Happy memories are the best shields against unhappy days."

T.M. Cicinski

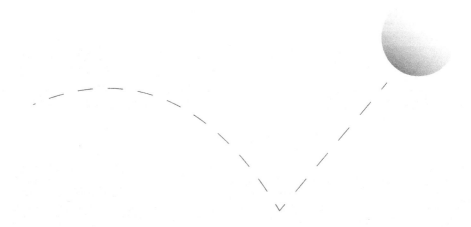

Chapter Ten

Remembering the Good

"I'm going to ask you to share your loss stories and what you're hoping to get out of this group," the grief counselor, Lisa, said. "We aren't going to go in any order but speak up like popcorn. Share your story when you're ready, or don't share at all. I've had people come to grief groups for the entire ten sessions and never say a thing. That's okay."

The room, filled with about a dozen grievers, went silent. Lisa waded in, "Anyone want to go first?"

Then, the stories spilled forth. Most of the attendees lost their loved ones years ago, and each time they told their stories, I cried a little for my own.

"Now that we've shared our stories," Lisa said, "I want to take a moment to ask what you noticed."

Several people raised their hands and made comments, but they didn't seem to offer what Lisa was looking for. I raised my hand. "Yes?" she said.

"No story was the same, but we all have felt hopeless and lonely. And we want to move on."

"Yes. Exactly. Grief comes in all shapes and sizes, but the impact on the person is similar. And because of that similarity, some tools can help – two of which I'll give you now."

Always a good student, I picked up my pen and opened my notebook.

"One of the tools to use when you're down is to change your location. Go outside or to another room. It's amazing how a new space can lighten the mood."

"Kind of what we used to do for our kids when they had the croup. We would take them outside," I said.

Lisa nodded before continuing, "Second, try to connect to your loved ones through happy memories. We will focus on that next meeting. Your assignment will be to bring a picture of your loved one and tell us about them. What were they like? How did they connect with you? What made you love them?"

She watched as a few of us wrote down the assignment, and then she stood up and said, "Our time is up. If you need to reach me, please email or call. See you next week."

We burst from the room, and those who could sprinted to their cars. It was like being released from a class we hated but needed in order to graduate.

I wondered if I ever would.

*   *   *

The idea of embracing the happy memories of Mario and my mother felt impossible then. I was still stuck in the moment I lost them – with all the feelings of regret, guilt, and trauma.

That's where many of us get trapped, and it doesn't have to be that way.

We need to embrace the "and." This was a tragic loss, *and* I can walk outside, stand in the sun, and feel better. The last days with

Mario were horrible, *and* I can choose to focus on all the happy memories I had with him instead.

Rewiring Our Brains

We are wired to focus on our negative[3] experiences, interactions, or thoughts. It's instinctual – our programming is such that we believe the thoughts will prevent us from harm. It's a bad habit – and we can break it. We can rewire our brains and focus on positive memories instead.

This is difficult because misery loves company. No matter how well-meaning people may be, many love to talk about the worst, especially when our lives are difficult. This can feel good and maybe even cause us to soak up their attention.

But it can also keep us from focusing on the good. After Mario died, my social anxiety hit an all-time high. I would try to keep it together at work, and then someone would ask me about Mario's family, which would spiral me downward for the rest of the day. But if I focused on something positive and forgot the loss briefly, I felt guilty. Grieving people don't laugh, right?

During an Emotional Freedom Technique (EFT) treatment, my practitioner, Sandra, said, "Try to connect to Mario through happy memories. You don't have to connect to him through sadness. You don't have to be sad to remember him. You can be happy thinking of him."

After I mentioned how much I struggled with that, she said, "I'm from Sicily. In my country, they dress widows in black and make people stay alone in mourning until they die. But you don't have to follow Mario to the grave. You're young. You can live."

We all can live, and focusing on positive memories is a life-affirming way to move forward.

When Happy Memories Aren't Available

It's important to note that there are times when it isn't possible to get to the happy memories. The trauma from the loss or event is so deep that it takes some form of therapy to address it. If this resonates with you, please get in touch with a therapist specializing in PTSD (also, the EFT technique mentioned previously is beneficial).

There are also times when there are no good memories available. I recently read the novel, *Burst*, by Mary Otis. It's about a complicated mother/daughter relationship. The mother could be categorized as a narcissist (although Otis never calls her that).

She is the sole source of influence over her daughter's upbringing, and her drinking and self-centered behavior simultaneously drive her daughter away and glue her to her mom's orbit.

Just as the adult daughter begins to rebuild their relationship, her mother dies. At the end of the story, the daughter takes the first step to integrate the happy memories of her mother into her life, and she begins to heal.

I cried a lot after reading the last chapter of the book. Integrating the happy memories of my mother is something I've only started to do.

When we lose someone difficult or something (like a job) that is challenging, it's a special case of grief. The feelings of resentment help us in the early days of loss. They give us a bit of cover and can mask our pain.

But it always catches up with us. I thought I was handling my mother's death well until my fiancé died three months later, leaving me a widow (of sorts). None of my friends or family could relate to what I was experiencing. The only one who could have – my mother – was also dead. This fed my resentment of her. Yet again, she wasn't there for me when I needed her.

But after reading *Burst* and having the cry I sorely needed, I found that I was ready to integrate happy memories of my mother.

Sadly, at first, only one happy memory came to mind. It was from my high school days. I was tasked with successfully baking a cheese soufflé and writing a paper about it. The recipe called for expensive ingredients, which my mother complained about. And since I couldn't get the soufflé to rise, I was afraid to tell her I needed to return to the grocery store. Yet, when I did, instead of yelling at me for wasting money, she took me to the store to purchase the ingredients and helped me get the recipe right. The soufflé rose, and her unexpected kindness stuck with me. She even stayed up and helped me type my paper because she was a better typist. Just thinking about that memory softens my heart toward her.

Then, on a recent museum visit in Milan, Italy, I had another happy memory (even though my mother sadly never visited Europe).

One crisp morning, after shuffling through multiple sealed rooms, we were led into a very long chapel. On one end were ten benches in front of Leonardo da Vinci's painting, "The Last Supper." I don't know if it was the quiet church setting (so familiar to my childhood)

"When integrating the loss of difficult people or situations, it's helpful to add an *and* to remember their positive aspects – because we can hold two feelings at once."

Donna Y. Ferris

or the painting's content, but a memory of my mother's love for it rushed in. It felt as if she was right there beside me, and together we experienced awe and gratitude for that moment. I couldn't help but cry from the joy and longing as I remembered that part of her.

Later, while sharing cheesecake with my husband after dinner, I remembered her telling a story about having New York City cheesecake on one of her first dates with my father.

How many times had I blocked these memories and many more because they were locked in the vault of resisting all things related to my mother? How much of my life story had I discarded or denied because I wouldn't allow more than one dimension of her to be true?

We can't change negative memories about people once they are out of our lives, but we can change how the memories affect us. And it's important to try – as focusing on the negative memories inadvertently blocks the loving, healthy ones.

Embracing the *And*

As mentioned earlier in the chapter, when integrating the loss of difficult people or situations, it's helpful to add an *and* to remember their positive aspects – because we can hold two feelings at once. For example:

My mother was an abuser *and* fierce in her support of righteous causes.

My mother was unkind to me *and* tenacious in pursuing whatever she wanted.

My mother was notorious for talking behind people's backs *and* a force to be reckoned with when her loved ones were wronged.

My mother was prickly *and* loved hard the only way she knew how.

I do miss my mother. She couldn't be the mother I needed, *and* there is much to admire in how she pushed through life.

Integrate the Loss

Acknowledging and integrating all our losses – even the less-than-lovable ones is important. There are good moments in every problematic situation. Including those memories is a more honest and fully dimensional look at the stories of our past.

This technique works for any challenging situation – bosses, jobs, marriages, ex-husbands. Every situation or person put in our path is there to teach us something.

List the difficult people in your life and what they've taught you. Seeing these positive aspects helps us tell a new, more complete story about our lives. This practice changes us from victim to survivor to triumphant thriver.

I would never have become a successful relationship manager if I hadn't felt like I was walking on broken glass as a child. Then, the only way to be safe was to make my mother happy. Again, I wish this never happened, but there's no question that the experience helped me in my career. (Now, I need to become more comfortable letting things be as they are.)

Of course, it's always easier to find positive memories to lift us when the person we love is or was loving. But when that isn't the case, it can take time to find those *ands*. Nevertheless, they are there.

Maybe the only way to let go of the power difficult people or situations wield over our lives is to find those happier memories.

All of our experiences contribute to our growth and help us find our life purpose. Read on to the next chapter to learn more about pursuing your purpose and creating the life you desire.

Journaling Exercise

Write down any good memories about the person or thing you lost. Note what that situation taught you. This applies to people, jobs, relationships, locations, etc. Create *and* statements. Notice if you feel a release when you can find good things about challenging relationships or situations. You might even create a picture board of happy memories from photos or pictures of places.

Meditation

Try the Good Memories Meditation at donnayferris.com/meditations.

Heart Chakra, Color and Crystals

The heart chakra may be helpful for this chapter. This chakra is the fourth energy center at the chest's center. It is associated with the color green or pink, and it governs emotions, compassion, love, and connection. It acts as a bridge between the lower and upper chakras, balancing an individual's physical and spiritual characteristics. Crystals and gems like rose quartz, green aventurine, and emerald are commonly used to open and balance the heart chakra.

Affirmations

Embrace the happy memories.
I'm thankful for what I had and what I still have.
I don't need to get stuck in my negative memories.
Everyone has *ands* in their life.
There is always something positive to remember.
I breathe in peace and acceptance.
As the intensity of my grief changes, love will remain.
I'm stronger than I know.
I think of my lost loved one with gratitude.
I'm a better person for the love I've known.

JOURNAL

"My response to
anything that happens,
good or bad,
is to keep making things.
Keep making art."

Taylor Swift

Chapter Eleven

Create Your Life

Burned out in my career and inspired by the movie *Under the Tuscan Sun* (based on the memoir by Frances Mayes), I used my airline miles to travel to Italy over a decade ago. My then-husband hated traveling, so I took my oldest daughter – who thankfully does.

While in Rome, I saw a bracelet in the window of a tiny shop on a cobblestone street. It had the words, "La fantasia e' piu' importante del sapere" on it. I had no idea what it meant – so I asked the shopkeeper for a translation:

"Imagination is more important than knowledge."

The author? Albert Einstein.

Despite it being more expensive than I hoped, I bought the bracelet and wore it all the time while dreaming of a creative life that didn't leave me fried (at the time, the only artistic thing I did each year was create our holiday card).

A few months ago, while editing this book, I revisited Italy with my new husband (who loves to travel). Not every part of my life (or that trip) is rosy (it turns out you *can* eat too much pasta), but with practice, I mostly see the positive rather than drown in daily annoyances, disappointments, and imperfections.

How did I create this life? One dream, intention, and habit change at a time.

Eulogy Goals Over Resume Goals

How do you think about your life? Do you look for approval outside of yourself? Does your career, relationship, and status define your success? Is that definition of success the primary source of your self-worth and happiness?

If you said yes, you are not alone. Our culture pushes us to believe that our car, house, marriage, or stock options will make us happy. But when we get what we thought we wanted, it still isn't enough. Maybe we need a healthy reframe like:

- Work is how I make a living.
- Relationships do not define me.
- The only approval I need is from myself.
- I define what success means to me.
- Happiness/satisfaction is an inside job.
- I can create the boundaries to have it all.
- My job isn't who I am but how I express who I am.

We need to turn our resume goals into eulogy goals. Why is it important to try? Because we will regret it if we don't. Here are the top five regrets[14] people have on their deathbed:

- "I wish I dared to live a life true to myself, not the life others expected of me."
- "I wish I didn't work so hard."
- "I wish I expressed my true feelings."
- "I wish I stayed in touch with my friends."
- "I wish I let myself be happier."

What Do You Want to Do with Your Life?

Why don't we let ourselves have what we want? One of Mary Oliver's most famous poems is "The Summer Day." The poem ends with a call to action, urging readers to embrace life and its opportunities enthusiastically and purposefully. It was published when she was fifty-five years old.

She was just hitting her stride.

What do you want to do with the rest of your life? What is your true calling? What would you do if you removed the word "failure" from your vocabulary and stopped worrying about it?

What if success is a life where you show up as your genuine divine self and can pursue what you were meant to?

Turning Trials Into Triumphs

Now that you've broken open and are on the mend, how will what you've gone through change your life? What is your true calling? Buddhists call this Dharma, or what we were put on the earth to do. The idea also appears in other wisdom texts like the Bible, "Each of you should use whatever gift you have received to serve others, as faithful stewards of God's grace in its various forms" (1 Peter 4:10-11). This idea is also discussed in author and psychologist Stephen Cope's *The Great Work of Your Life – A Guide for the Journey to Your True Calling*. (I highly recommend it.)

Where can you find clues to your life purpose? Turn to your journaling pages and answer these questions (inspired in part by Cope's book):

- **What are your skills?**
  - ° What do you feel most confident doing?
  - ° Are there activities you enjoy more than others?
  - ° Have you received positive feedback or recognition for any capabilities?
- **What are your core values?**
  - ° Think about people you admire. What qualities in them resonate with you?
  - ° Reflect on instances when you felt a strong emotional reaction. What values might have been in play in those situations?
  - ° Consider your reactions to injustice or unfairness. What values might you hold that are being violated in those situations?
- **What do you love to do? Without censoring, make a list.**
  - ° If you have a free day, how would you spend it?
  - ° What activities make you forget about time?
  - ° What would you make or create and give away for free?
- **In what ways do you sense a responsibility to support others?**
  - ° It's that thing you will regret on your deathbed if you don't do it.
- **Who inspires you?**
  - ° Are there aspects of their character or achievements you aspire to incorporate into your life?

- How has this person overcome challenges or adversity?
- Do you find inspiration in people from different walks of life, or is there a specific field that resonates with you or a group you'd like to serve?
- **What do you want to share with the world because of what you've been through?**
  - What unique story do you have to tell?
  - What would you do if you had no excuses?

Look at what you wrote. As you read the words, what do you feel in your body and where? If you feel it in your heart, you're on your way!

Time Audit

Whenever I get to this part of a *Create Your Life* workshop or speech, someone raises their hand and says, "But I haven't got the time."

I always respond with "time audit!" This involves writing down everything you do for two days. I guarantee you will find small blocks of open time where you can pursue your dream. Even twenty-five minutes daily is enough to write a first book draft in four months (500 words in twenty-five minutes a day x 120 days = a 60,000-word book = 120 days). If that is the math, and you want to share your story with others, why aren't you doing it?

What is your dream?

You are what you pay attention to. Are you paying attention to your dream? Or are you filling your mind with social media, gaming, shopping, and news? Do these activities support your desires?

For helpful inspiration, I watch underdog stories like *Creed* (his line, "I'm not a mistake" gets me every time) and TV series like *Jann, Hacks,* or *Home Town* or *Bargain Block* on HGTV. I also like books about strong women overcoming no-win situations like *Lessons in Chemistry* and mysteries solved by unlikely sleuths like *A Good Girl's Guide to Murder.* (A list of these and other favorite inspirations is in the back of this book.)

They all reaffirm this mantra: "I have the power to overcome anything and create the life I want."

Really.

You just need an intention that supports your dream and a small commitment each day. You never know how far it will take you.

That's how I got to a healthier weight, stayed sober, and wrote my first book. By breaking down the intention into small, healthy bites like walking daily, staying dry one day at a time, and writing for twenty-five minutes each morning. Or as the author of *Maybe You Should Talk to Someone*, Lori Gottlieb, says, "Most big transformations come about from the hundreds of tiny, almost imperceptible, steps we take along the way."

"I have the power
to overcome anything
and create the
life I want."

Donna Y. Ferris

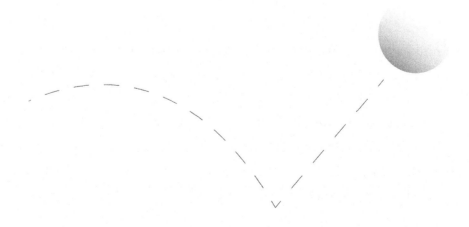

It's Up to You

When you're nearing the end of your life and look back, what do you want to have accomplished? What small actions can you take to get there?

It isn't easy. But if we learned anything from the pandemic years, this is the time to do what we're called to, despite fears of failure. If we aren't going to do it now, then when?

It doesn't mean you have to quit your day job. Here is a list of people who pursued their life purpose and still had a day job to pay the bills until they could pay those bills with their dream:

- John Legend
- T.S. Eliot
- Sara Blakely
- Steve Wozniak
- Scott Adams
- Donna Y. Ferris
- Insert your name here_____

May It Be of Benefit

For Christmas one year, my husband gave me a book by Viktor Frankl after I mentioned liking several of his quotes. Although this may not be a typical book to give as a gift, it was perfect for me.

Viktor Frankl was a psychiatrist who survived four Nazi concentration camps, only to discover, upon escape, that he'd lost his entire family in them. The book he wrote as a result, *Man's Search for Meaning*, was initially meant to be published anonymously. Frankl never wanted to be famous. He just wanted to share how he and others had survived their horrific experience.

The book has sold more than 15 million copies worldwide.

I started reading it, and within an hour, I had cried more than once. The work is broken into two parts. The first describes the concentration camp experience, and the second explains how he and others survived. I found myself reading a few pages from the first part and then turning to the second quickly for relief. I repeated this over and over.

How did he survive? By finding meaning in his life. He wrote a manuscript that he believed to be his life's work, but it was discarded in one of the camps. Reconstructing it helped to sustain him through his ordeal. Later, after publishing more than thirty books, he said the true meaning of his life was to help others find the meaning of theirs – to be of benefit.

I've seen this in my own life as well. I was devastated when I experienced repeated losses (divorce and death) over three years. I felt like that spider of nursery rhyme lore, crawling up the waterspout, only to get washed down over and over. I wrote about my grief journey in articles and my memoir. Each instance gave me distance, perspective, and a community of others going through the same thing. Writing provided a purpose and helped me see suffering as a part of life. It gave me much-needed context and stopped me from taking blessings and others for granted.

How might *you* continually find meaning and purpose in your life? Seek ways to be creative, interact with others, and turn your suffering into benefit?

If Viktor could do it, we all can.

It just takes a little faith and surrender. More on that in the next chapter.

Journaling Exercise

Complete the questions on pages 172-173. Now what would you do if you couldn't fail? What is your stretch goal? Write it down, take one mini step or SMART (specific, measurable, achievable, realistic, timely) goal toward it at least five days a week for a month, and see what happens.

Meditation

Try the Create Your Life Meditation at donnayferris.com/meditations.

Sacral Chakra, Color and Crystals

The sacral chakra is the second energy center located in the lower abdomen, just below the navel. This chakra is represented by the color orange, and is associated with creativity, sensuality, and emotional expression. The sacral chakra influences one's ability to experience pleasure and connect with others on an emotional level. Crystals like Carnelian, Orange Calcite, and Moonstone are commonly used to balance and stimulate this chakra.

Affirmations

I have the power to overcome anything and create the life I want.

I'm grateful for all I've learned.

Today is filled with possibilities.

I'm strong enough to overcome challenges.

I do my best to accomplish my goals.

I have strengths, abilities, and gifts.

All that's possible for anyone is possible for me.

I attract positive things and people into my life.

My ideas are worth being shared.

I'm worthy and deserving of all the things I want in my life.

"Great people do things before they're ready. They do things before they know they can do it."

Amy Poehler

Chapter Twelve

If You Don't Like the Word Faith, Then F*ck it

I recently heard famous meditation teacher, Sharon Salzberg, say on a podcast that her least successful book is *Faith*. She was advised not to use that title because of a concern that the public has an aversion to religious terms.

But she went ahead anyway.

She went forward on faith.

This is what we all have to do at some point. We must commit to a path, do our best, and surrender the outcome. We release attachment to whatever may come. We trust in ourselves, the Universe (or our higher power), life's inherent goodness, and the human spirit.

No Excuses

In the last year of my first marriage, I finally accepted a previously declined invitation to go to a yoga retreat at the Stockbridge, Massachusetts facility called Kripalu Center for

Yoga and Health. After my first yoga class there, I told a group of strangers in a sharing circle about my childhood abuse. It was the first time I'd shared this personal shame publicly. Afterward, at a *No Excuses* workshop, I picked yoga teacher training as the thing I wanted to do, no matter the roadblock. I had no idea why I picked it or how it would fit into my busy work and family life. I just knew I had to do it.

I acted on *faith*.

That one act launched me on a path that supported me through all the challenges that followed – my divorce, loss of my mother, loss of Mario, and my youngest child's transition.

That trip was a "yolo" (you only live once) move that changed my life. It led to a one-year yoga teacher training, a three-year yoga therapy training, Reiki training, writing my memoir, and much more.

All of these were leaps of faith.

Or as social scientist Arthur Brooks says, "Faith is anything transcendent that helps you escape the boring sitcom that is your life."

Surrender

Maybe faith isn't your word. Perhaps the idea of leaning on a higher power bothers you.

I've had as challenging a religious past as any, and it wasn't until I got back on a spiritual path that everything in my life came together.

But for those still squeamish about the word faith, maybe another phrase like "f*ck it" is better.

Think about it – the sentiment is similar. "I'm not sure how this will work out, but what the heck, I'm going to do it anyway." It's another form of faith. I've tried everything else, and now it's time to leap.

Whatever you call it, life requires a bit of surrender.

I used to tense up when I heard the word "surrender." I'd think, "I'm not going to surrender to anything or anyone! I'm a winner, not a loser!"

But what surrender means in this context is that we've done our best, and the rest is in the hands of our higher power.

Give it a try. Think of something you've taken as far as you can. Maybe it's a project, a child's problem, your loss recovery, or a health scare. If you've put everything into it, give it over through prayer or meditation. Or maybe write down your desire on paper and lay it under a full moon (you can also burn it). You've done your best, and it's time to leave the next "bit" to the universe (or higher power).

How does it feel when you surrender the outcome? Is there a softening or release in your chest or forehead? Do you find it easier to walk, breathe, or sleep?

Isn't it all out of our hands anyway? Like in The Mind Game chapter, our mental attachments to outcomes are our way of trying to control or make sense of the world. They aren't real. We can't orchestrate what happens to us. The only thing we have agency over is our reactions – what we do with what's happened to us.

That is where our true power lies.

Maybe the Best Way to Help Others is to Model Healthy Behavior

Anyone who has a child in their life knows that kids model our *behavior*. My daughter said, "Oh sh*t," by age three, even though I told her it wasn't okay to swear. She said it because that's what I did when I was frustrated.

Adults are the same. We watch what others do. We can say as much as we want, but people will remember what we do. Or as Maya Angelou famously said, "I've learned that people will forget what you said, people will forget what you did, but people will never forget how you made them feel."

Our interactions with others and how we make them feel are our most significant contributions to the world. That's why it's so important to be our best selves – and to lead with love instead of fear. We can do this through meditation and other self-care practices.

And if you take a step each day to be a little happier, lifted, and inspired, you will be your best self. It will all work out. Inspiration around what to do next will come, along with unexpected assistance.

Let Life Flow

You may not get exactly what you want, but as the Rolling Stones said, you'll get what you need.

"Our interactions with others and how we make them feel are our most significant contributions to the world. That's why it's so important to be our best selves – and to lead with love instead of fear."

Donna Y. Ferris

There's magic in the serendipity of a higher power that inserts help at the perfect time. Some people call it happenstance. Others call it divine intervention or grace. In the movie *Elf*, they call it Christmas spirit.

No matter the name, as we near the end of this book, it's wise to acknowledge that sometimes, nothing works. All we can do is get out of the way and let life flow.

If you're facing one of those times when you can't see the next step or imagine there could be another sunrise, faith (or f*ck it) may be precisely all that's left.

Trust me, it'll be enough.

This brings us to the next chapter, where we'll reflect on the lessons challenges offer, and how writing about them helps us heal.

Journaling Exercise

What are your beliefs about faith and surrender? Have you ever left your next step in the hands of a higher power? How would it feel to do that now? Try the meditation for this chapter, and write down any ideas of next steps that come to you, even if they feel incredibly far-fetched. Pursue one, and see what happens.

Meditation

Try the Surrender Meditation at donnayferris.com/meditations.

Crown Chakra, Color, and Crystals

The crown chakra is the seventh and highest energy center and is located at the top of the head. Symbolized by the color violet or white, this chakra represents spiritual connection, divine consciousness, and enlightenment. It serves as the gateway to higher states of awareness and understanding. Crystals such as amethyst, clear quartz, and selenite are often used to balance and activate the crown chakra.

Affirmations

I don't have to make everything happen.
I let go of what I can't change.

Regardless of the outcome, the Universe/God takes care of me.

The Universe/God has a plan greater than mine.

Trust the process.

I am open and willing to live my life in new ways.

Sometimes I can get out of the way and let the Universe/God take over.

I feel peaceful knowing I'm where I'm supposed to be.

I have done my best; it's time to surrender the outcome.

I relinquish control and surrender to a higher power.

JOURNAL

JOURNAL

"If there's anything
in your life you want
to change, then it's time
to adjust the story
you tell about yourself."

Colette Baron-Reid

Chapter Thirteen

Writing Our Way to Healing

The words came at me like a hailstorm, but the sound of my thumping heart made it hard to concentrate. Then one word registered.

"Attacked."

The ear of my beloved rescue Jake was torn in two, and a clump of dark blood showed at the seams. He'd been attacked by a beagle half his size at the pet sitter after the smaller dog was stung by a bee.

Jake's leash was limp in my hands as the sitter told the story. But aside from the wound, Jake seemed fine.

I was a wreck.

Later, my vet had to write down simple antibiotic instructions because my shocked brain couldn't compute.

Jake and I had weathered every one of my recent tragedies together. He'd always been there for me. Yet, when he needed me, I was 360 miles away, taking my daughter to college.

This incident had all the *things* – a being I love, guilt over not being there, and the fear of losing him.

Yet what did Jake when we got home? He sat quietly in the grief chair I bought after Mario's death.

I would've loved to sit in that comfy blue chair and wallow, but Jake secured it as his own the day I got it six years ago and rarely is out of it. It's like he knows it's a bad idea for me to burrow, and he won't have it.

My oldest daughter called me after I texted her the news, and when I told her how distraught I was, she said, "What are you going to do for yourself, Mom?

It's a gift when our lessons spring from our children's mouths.

So I started writing. That's what I do to take care of myself. It's a way to bring order to the commotion in my mind. When I figure out how to write about it, I witness the situation rather than embody it.

If you have the same instinct, follow it.

Why Write?

We write to understand what we think and to tell the story our way. We write to remember who we are. We also write to make a difference.

It isn't a practice to be finished, but a way to understand our life and place in it. Before writing my first book, I'd been writing a suspense novel for almost a decade (see an excerpt from this soon-to-be-published work in the back of this book). I even had a first draft. But then, my life fell apart, and I felt compelled to write about that instead – first in blogs, then a memoir. Then, I started this book based on what

I learned from those experiences.

When I hit publish on that first blog eight years ago, I wasn't thinking it would help me heal. I did it because I couldn't stop. Instinctively, I knew it would help.

Now, of course, I understand that writing (or any activity that, as Brené Brown says, "…makes you forget about time.") helps when we face difficulties. When the wheels come off the bus or when one of your precious hound's ears is torn to shreds.

Those ears.

All dogs can sense energy, but this dog is gifted empathetically. When Jake meets someone with kind energy, his ears spread like he's about to take flight. Whenever he reacted that way to someone, I told them how special he thought they were. But when I dropped him off at the vet for ear repair surgery, I was sure this would never happen again.

And once Jake got home from the vet, *he* didn't whimper once about his ear.

Ironic, right? This dog was the injured party, but I was the one who couldn't stop sobbing.

That's what writing does. It gives us space to witness our behavior. It lets us inject irony, humor, and wisdom. Let's us express the roiling energy in our bodies and transform it into something of benefit. (Of course, other creative activities are beneficial too, like painting, drawing, dancing, cooking, singing, decorating, and gardening.)

And just in case you're wondering – thanks to the amazing efforts of my vet – Jake's ear is back to its role as a kindness meter.

Why I No Longer Call My Mother A Narcissist

A funny thing happened on the way to publishing this book. I gave the manuscript to my sister to give feedback. And she took issue with me calling our mother a narcissist.

At first, I was stubbornly determined to go forward with the characterization. I had a list of why's all teed up.

And then realized I was putting my mother in a trendy box. I was propagating a story in which she was evil, and my dad was good. But my siblings were treated differently by my mom and have a different view of her – and some found Dad more difficult. What's the truth? Probably all of it. And maybe there was something about me, or a contributing situation, that caused her to mistreat me. I can't ask her now. But dumping her into the narcissist bucket doesn't allow for any of those nuances or complexities. And it took writing this book and asking for feedback to reach this realization – and acceptance.

That, dear readers, is what writing does. It gives us distance, context, connection – and maybe most importantly – healing.

How Do We Write Our Way to Healing?

It's okay if you don't share your stories. Writing them down is enough. And you don't have to write well. It isn't about that. It's about letting the energy and feelings flow so they don't keep us stuck.

"You don't have to write well. It isn't about that. It's about letting the energy and feelings flow so they don't keep us stuck."

Donna Y. Ferris

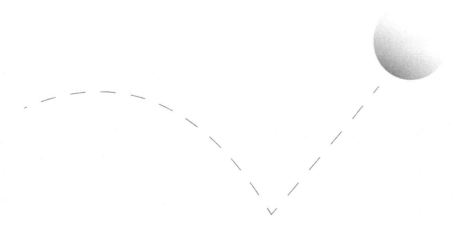

Start with a daily journaling practice. *In The Artist's Way*, author Julia Cameron suggests we write morning pages longhand, and they can be about absolutely anything . . . or nothing. Set a timer for twenty-five minutes, and let it all out. Then, read what you've written. Did you learn anything new?

Another book I've found incredibly helpful in unlocking blocks to creativity is *Yoga for the Creative Soul* by Erin Byron. One of her suggestions to help write about our difficult times is to create a comfortable place and a calming presence (through one or more of the self-care habits discussed in Chapter Four) – and then listen to a song you hate. As you hear the uncomfortable notes, let the feelings rise and fall, maybe after a time, dance with the feelings. I've found this exercise incredibly helpful in building a tolerance for uncomfortable moments so I can write my way through them and release their sting.

Sharing Our Stories

You can always keep these stories to yourself. But if you do want to share them, there are multiple formats for this effort, including:

- Opinion pages and print or online magazines, which take pieces of 750-1,000 words in length. Start with your story, then weave in wisdom or lists of to-dos to address the situation. Focus on being of benefit to the reader. This is a great way to build an audience and chip away at a longer work. Before submitting, look at the outlet's writing guidelines and requirements.

- Newsletters, which are helpful for building an email list. I publish a newsletter monthly with a blog (which forms chapters for my books), TV/movie reviews, book reviews, and a list of upcoming speaking, workshop, and retreat events. To subscribe to this newsletter, email me at donna@donnayferris.com.

- Podcasts are another way to process happenings in your life for the benefit of others. As noted in the first bullet, you will likely start with an outline based on something that happened to you and end with advice and to-dos. That is why I started my podcast *Bounce Back Stronger*[15]. There are plenty of books and primers on starting a podcast. I would start with Matty Dalrymple's book, *Podcasting for Authors*.

- Memoirs are a fantastic way to work through trauma or difficult periods, and the best book on doing that is *The Art of Memoir* by Mary Karr.

- Novels are another way to tell our stories. Most authors pull from real life for these fictional works. They change characters and schematic elements, but the feelings and situations come from their lives. There are many books, courses, and podcasts on this subject. One of my favorites is *Anatomy of a Bestseller* by Sacha Black and the *Creative Penn* podcast by Joanna Penn.

If you want to pursue writing, I lead writing retreats and workshops and provide writing coaching. Reach out to me at donna@donnayferris.com if you're interested in learning more.

One of the most critical outcomes of writing our way to healing may be that by sharing it, others benefit. They may even ask you how you made it through (this warms my heart every time it happens). As a result, we are all less alone and feel the universe's embrace.

You've Already Started

Throughout this book, you've had opportunities to journal and reshape how you think about your stories. And now, you can mold your writings into something beneficial for others. It isn't a requirement, but an opportunity if you so choose. Even if you only share it with one person, the outcome will be transformative for you both.

Only two more chapters to go, so there's no time like the present. How will you write your way to healing?

"And when we get to where we're going, turn around and help her too. For there was a time not so long ago when she was you."
~Anonymous

Journaling Exercise

Set a twenty-five-minute timer each day for a week, and write your thoughts. Include at least one thing you are grateful for, and increase that to three things, if you can. Notice what happens over a week, month, or year when you do this for at least five days each week.

Meditation

Try the Five Senses Writing Meditation at donnayferris.com/meditations.

Throat Chakra, Color, and Crystals

The throat chakra is the fifth energy center situated at the throat region. Symbolized by the color blue, this chakra governs communication, self-expression, and the ability to speak one's truth. (I intentionally wear blue when I have to present or communicate something important.) Crystals like Blue Lace Agate, Sodalite, and Aquamarine are commonly used to balance and activate the throat chakra.

Affirmations

Writing is healing.

My words are worth making time for.

I don't have to wait for inspiration; I just have to show up.

I have a story to tell, and it will be of benefit to others.

My words matter.

I have the power to create something beautiful.

My words don't have to be perfect to be worthy and meaningful.

The infinite power of the Universe/God flows through my fingertips.

The world needs the magic inside of me.

I can write my way to healing.

JOURNAL

"I've discovered that grief means living with someone who is not there."

Jeanette Winterson

Chapter Fourteen

The Holidays
(and other difficult days)

I don't know exactly when it started.

Was it last night when I needed to watch *White Christmas*? Or was it the Facebook pop-up of Mario's last holiday?

Some days, grief sneaks up on me, but around holidays (or other difficult days like birthdays or anniversaries), I see it coming. Sometimes weeks beforehand.

The sadness seeps into every bone, and then I realize I'm waist-deep.

With experience, I know what to do and lean on these tools and mental strategies. Sometimes, I need one – other times, it takes them all:

- **ANTICIPATION IS USUALLY WORSE THAN REALITY –** Realizing the day itself may go easier than we think is helpful. Like waiting for a dentist appointment, the anticipation of how the day will be is usually way worse than it is. Knowing this can smooth the sting of the days and weeks prior.

- **MAKE A PLAN –** It's helpful to plan some way to commemorate the day and honor those we've lost. Maybe it's visiting their final resting place or going to a park or location you enjoyed together. For me, this involves a cup of Wawa French vanilla coffee and a drive over to a nearby park where a tree was planted in Mario's memory. I walk around it and tell him about the kids and what we're doing for the holiday. Sometimes, I see a new tree in the grove and send peaceful wishes to those who planted it.

- **BE READY TO DITCH THE PLAN –** Sometimes, our plans don't work. We wake up too sad or low energy. This is okay. Listen to your body and do what you can to get through the day – maybe by doing the next thing on this list.

- **WRITE OR DO SOMETHING CREATIVE –** My go-to is writing or working on my podcast, latest book, or monthly newsletter. These activities take my attention and ensure I'm doing something useful with my feelings. Other creative ideas include cooking, painting, doing a puzzle, or wrapping presents. Whatever brings joy and creative distraction.

- **TRY TO REFRAIN FROM ANYTHING DESTRUCTIVE –** I didn't do so well at this recently. When I went to the grocery store for our weekly haul, I bought a large bag of kettle corn and later ate most of it in front of the TV. (Before becoming sober, I would have drunk a bottle of wine, so I give myself a slight pass for the popcorn. But threw the rest of it away the next day.)

- **DECLUTTER OR RE-ARRANGE A ROOM OR YOUR LIFE –** Reorient a desk or a seating place to face a window. This allows new energy to enter the space. Even emptying and re-ordering a drawer or closet is enough to shift our energy and lift our spirits.

- **LOSE YOURSELF IN SOMETHING –** Flipping through Netflix, I found the TV show *So Help Me Todd*. It was the perfect combination of humor, action, and surprise to distract me.

- **GO TO BED EARLY –** Sometimes, a good night's sleep is all that's required. On holidays I make sure to eat a light dinner early (because big meals late can derail slumber) and take a long hot bath. Then, I crawl into bed with a lighthearted read and stay there for the duration.

- **MEDITATE AND/OR PRAY EARLY AND OFTEN –** It's helpful to take a break from our thoughts by meditating or praying. Leaving the feelings with a higher power or the universe can be a relief.

- **BELIEVE IN MAGIC –** Our loved ones are not gone forever. Their energy lives on and visits us from time to time in the form of cardinals, songs on the radio, or unexpected calls or texts from friends and family when we need them.

The love we have for those we've lost outlives the physical form. It never dies. We just need to believe in it and them.

I hope you do – and that these tools and those in earlier chapters help you in all the days ahead.

"The love we have for those we've lost outlives the physical form. It never dies. We just need to believe in it and them."

Donna Y. Ferris

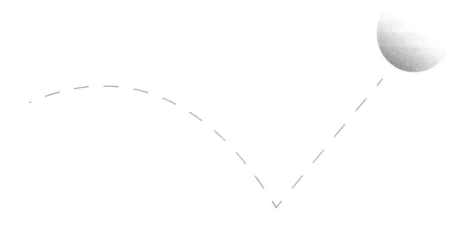

Journaling Exercise

Develop a plan for the holidays or other special days. Don't be afraid to throw it out or make a new one if that feels right.

Meditation

Try For the Difficult Days Meditation at donnayferris.com/meditations.

Root Chakra, Color and Crystals

The root chakra, located at the base of the spine, is the chakra most helpful for this chapter and the next. This chakra is the foundational energy center associated with survival, stability, and grounding. Represented by the color red, the root chakra's key aspects include physical health, security, and connection to the Earth. Crystals such as red jasper, hematite, black tourmaline, and black obsidian are believed to balance this chakra by fostering grounding and stability.

Affirmations:

I am allowing myself to grieve and heal today, understanding that it is a natural part of the process.

I believe in the enduring magic of love.

I am finding strength and resilience within myself to navigate this difficult day.

I am honoring my feelings of grief and allowing myself the space to heal in my own time.

I am embracing self-compassion as I navigate through the challenges of grief.

I am surrounded by love and support, and I allow myself to lean on others during this time of grief.

My heart is open to finding moments of joy and peace amid the pain of loss today.

I release any guilt associated with grieving today and grant myself permission to prioritize my well-being.

I am creating new traditions and rituals that honor the memory of my loved one while bringing comfort to my heart.

Through self-care and reflection, I am finding a sense of peace and acceptance today.

JOURNAL

"Everything will work out. It already has."

Erin Byron

Chapter Fifteen

Be a Bumble

One of my favorite Christmas traditions is watching *Rudolph the Red-Nosed Reindeer & the Island of the Misfit Toys,* particularly the scenes with the snow monster Bumble. Despite his daunting presence, Bumble transforms from scary menace to lovable hero after falling over a cliff and bouncing back. This event inspired the catchphrase, "Bumbles bounce."

Now it's your time to bounce. What you've experienced is difficult, even devastating, but it's also your greatest teacher. Our challenges remind us that life is too short to remain mired in a valley of despair. Instead, we can bravely bounce back by consciously viewing setbacks as a chance to create a more intentional and fulfilling life. Yes, it's hard, but it's also our life's work.

Once we consciously adopt a resilient persona, we can find peace and purpose no matter what happens. Every block becomes an opportunity – not on day one, but a day closer and closer to the first moment of heartbreak.

Eventually, we can model this enlightenment for others, and they will do the same for us when needed – and those on this path will surround us, and we can find the loving care and happiness we desire.

That is my hope for you.

If I can support you, let me know.

With that, let's close with the Metta meditation:

May you be happy.

May you be healthy.

May you be safe.

May you ride the waves of life with peace.

Love and light to you,

Donna

Journaling Exercise

Write down three things you are going to take away from this book. Pick one related action item that you are going to work on. Identify one small task you can do five times a week around this learning. Keep track of your progress in your journaling pages, and celebrate your achievements at the end of the week with something from your self-care list.

Also, note how your plant is doing today (only if this is relevant). How tall is it? Maybe even draw a picture or share it with friends or on social media. Celebrate how far you both have come.

Meditation

Pick your favorite meditation from those in this book. Look back and see which meditation you first picked after reading Chapter One. Are they the same or different? Note this down in your journaling pages and any thoughts about your choices. Listen to your favorite meditation at least five times in the next week. Keep track of your progress in your journaling pages, the mood and focus of the days you meditate, and celebrate your meditating achievements with something from your self-care list.

Chakra, Color, and Crystals

Which one speaks to you today? If you aren't sure, look back at the chakra discussions in each chapter and see if one calls out to you. Wear it as clothing, and find a way to inject it into your environment (flowers, plants, crystals, or pictures). See what happens.

Affirmations:

I am brave.

I am strong enough to overcome any obstacle.

I am grateful for the memories I share with my loved one. They will always be in my heart.

I have faith that everything will work out for my good.

I am capable of achieving my goals despite the obstacles I'm facing.

I choose to heal my hurt spirit and move on with grace.

I am brave and possess great courage. I go beyond my comfort zone and challenge my limits.

I am worthy of love and happiness. I deserve to be happy again.

I have the power within me to change my life for the better.

I am not alone. I have support and guidance from the Universe/God and my angels.

JOURNAL

Thank You for Reading

If you liked this book, please post a review on Amazon, Goodreads, and social media. Thank you.

If you want support for your journey, please visit donnayferris.com.

To obtain a free printable pdf of the coloring pages in this book please email donna@donnayferris.com or visit donnayferris.com/coloringpages.

Acknowledgments

My Dad died when I was twenty-five, and my life fell apart. He was the only parent who loved me unconditionally and believed in me. He said I would be the most spiritual of his children – even though I had recently received my MBA straight after undergrad and was pursuing a money-focused financial career hard.

After he died, I was lost and over-functioned for a time. I cared for my mother, took on a job with a required 80-hour work week, and fell into a marriage that felt safe. I leaned heavily on the book *How to Survive the Loss of a Love* and vowed to share what I learned with all my friends facing their own grief journeys, thinking I had it all figured out.

And here I am, over thirty years later, publishing this book, knowing that loss is one of life's biggest teachers, and it never stops giving.

This book encapsulates everything I've learned from my loss journey and in writing my memoir *We've Got to Stop Meeting Like This* and the related workshops and retreats that followed.

Thank you to all of my readers, students, clients, and podcast listeners for reading, following, and allowing me to be a part of your journey – especially Christine Bennett, Theresa Hoffman, Lydia Lampert, Patti Stromberg, and Sylvie Ashby.

Thank you to my copy editor, Kevin Ferris; developmental editor, Melanie Votaw; my sanity check editor, Beverly Wilkes; and cover and book designer, Amy Junod Placentra.

Thank you to Sharon Salzberg, Erin Byron, Cristina Leeson, Colleen Dixon, and Maria Sirois for their support and inspiration.

Special shout out to my siblings for their love and support no matter the distance between us.

Thank you to Samson, Yogi, Cooper, and Jake for their unconditional love and effortless ability to make us laugh.

Thank you to my therapist Renee Freilich - not sure where I'd be without your input in my life.

Thank you to my best friend, Joy. I am so grateful for your gentle guidance in my life.

Thank you to my dear children, who have taught me as much as I have them.

And finally, thank you to my beloved, Kevin, for showing me what it means to be kind, generous, and loving. I am blessed by every day we have together.

Resource List

Non-Fiction Books

Radical Acceptance: Embracing Your Life with the Heart of a Buddha – Tara Brach

The Gifts of Imperfection – Brené Brown

Yoga for the Creative Soul: Exploring the Five Paths of Yoga to Reclaim Your Expressive Spirit– Erin Byron

The Artist's Way: A Spiritual Path to Higher Creativity – Julia Cameron

When Things Fall Apart: Heart Advice for Difficult Times – Pema Chödrön

The Great Work of Your Life: A Guide for the Journey to Your True Calling – Stephen Cope

Devotions – Mary Oliver

Faith: Trusting Your Own Deepest Experience – Sharon Salzberg

Love Your Enemies: How to Break the Anger Habit & Be a Whole Lot Happier – Sharon Salzberg and Robert Thurman

Dipa Ma: The Life and Legacy of a Buddhist Master — Amy Schmidt

The Untethered Soul: The Journey Beyond Yourself – Michael A. Singer

A Short Course in Happiness After Loss (And Other Dark, Difficult Times) – Maria Sirois

The Body Keeps the Score: Brain, Mind, and Body in the Healing of Trauma – Bessel van der Kolk, MD

Meditation Apps / Sites

Insight Timer
Ten Percent Happier
donnayferris.com/meditations

Retreats / Workshops

Soak Up the Sun Retreats – donnayferris.com/events
Kripalu – www.kripalu.org

TV Shows

Bargain Block
Hacks
Home Town
Jann
Julia
So Help Me Todd
Ted Lasso

Movies

A Man Called Otto
Creed
Die Hard
Elf
Good Will Hunting
Julie and Julia
Princess Diaries (or pretty much anything with Julie Andrews)
Somewhere in Queens
The Best Exotic Marigold Hotel
The Holdovers
The Hundred-Foot Journey

Fiction Books

Wonder Walkers – Micha Archer
Finlay Donovan is Killing it – Elle Cosimano
Lessons in Chemistry – Bonnie Garmus
A Good Girl's Guide to Murder – Holly Jackson
The Only Girl in the Room – Donna Y Ferris (coming soon)
Remarkably Bright Creatures – Shelby Van Pelt
The House in the Cerulean Sea – TJ Klune

Bounce Back Stronger Playlist
(On Spotify)

"Don't You Worry 'Bout a Thing – Stevie Wonder

"With a Little Luck" – Paul McCartney

"Feels So Good" – Chuck Mangione

"You're the First, the Last, My Everything" – Barry White

"Little Wonders" – Rob Thomas

"Smile" – Uncle Kracker

"Don't Stop Believin'" - Journey

"Give a Little Bit" – Goo Goo Dolls

"Shower the People" – James Taylor

"Tubthumping" – Chumbawamba

"Back in the High Life" – Steve Winwood

"Moonshadow" – Cat Stevens

"Weightless" – Marconi Union

"What a Wonderful World" – Louis Armstrong

Endnotes

1 Ferris, Donna, *Bounce Back Stronger* podcast, Episode 2, https://podcasts.apple.com/us/podcast/the-science-of-resilience/id1716530620?i=1000634897970

2 Smith, Colleen, *Art & Object,* https://www.artandobject.com/articles/neuroaesthetics-how-art-scientifically-proven-help-brain-health

3 Thorpe, Matthew & Ajmera, Rachael, *Healthline,* https://www.healthline.com/nutrition/12-benefits-of-meditation

4 Pratt, Misty, *Mindful.org,* https://www.mindful.org/the-science-of-gratitude

5 Pratt, Misty, *Mindful.org,* https://www.mindful.org/the-science-of-gratitude

6 Ferris, Donna, *Elephant Journal,* https://www.elephantjournal.com/2021/08/the-one-thing-we-can-do-every-morning-to-make-us-3-percent-happier-donna-yates-ferris/

7 Aujla, Rupy, *The Doctor's Kitchen* podcast, https://thedoctorskitchen.com/podcasts/145-eating-for-mental-health-with-dr-rupy

8 Rogers, Kristen, *CNN*, https://www.cnn.com/2021/09/12/ health/five-stages-of-grief-kubler-ross-meaning-wellness/ index.html

9 Bradt, Steve, *The Harvard Gazette*, https://news.harvard. edu/gazette/story/2010/11/wandering-mind-not-a-happy- mind

10 Szuhany, Kristin & Malgaroli, Matteo & Miron, Carly & Simon, Naomi, *Psychiatry Online*, https://focus.psychiatryonline.org/doi/10.1176/appi. focus.20200052

11 White, Barry, *Ally McBeal*, https://youtu.be/UVcyrEYVfiM

12 West, Jennifer & Liang, Belle & Spinazolla, Joseph, *National Library of Medicine*, https://www.ncbi.nlm.nih.gov/ pmc/articles/PMC5404814

13 Black, David, *Lexipol*, https://www.cordico. com/2021/01/20/why-our-brains-fixate-on-the-bad-and- what-to-do-about-it

14 Pickering, James, *Old Colony Hospice*, https://www.oldcolonyhospice.org/blog/bid/101702/ nurse-reveals-the-top-five-regrets-people-make-on-their- deathbed

15 Ferris, Donna, *Bounce Back Stronger* podcast, https:// podcasts.apple.com/us/podcast/bounce-back-stronger- with-donna-ferris/id1716530620

COMING IN 2025

The Only Girl in the Room

BY DONNA Y. FERRIS

The first thing I heard was beeping.

High.

Shrill.

Pounding.

It seeped into my ears from far away – but grew closer and closer.

And then the pain descended. A stab at first, followed by a hammering ache. It centered on the back of my skull, then radiated down my spine. I'd never felt anything like it before.

The beeping sped up. I took a deep breath in. It slowed down.

What's that smell? Antiseptic mixed with bleach. Familiar. Wait – there's only one place with that combination. The beeping sped up.

My eyes opened. White. White walls, white lights, white sheets.

"No, no, no!" There's a tube taped to my arm connected to a clear plastic bag on a silver pole. As I pulled at the plastic edges holding the cylinder, a young woman in a blue smock yelled down the hall. Three people – a deliciously scented younger man, an older puffy-eyed one, and a smiling grey-haired hippie – circled the bed and started talking at once.

My heart beat in my throat. I had to get the IV out of my arm. I almost was free when a second nurse with a Snoopy smock and dark glasses rushed in.

She started reapplying the tape, "Miss Barnett, you need that." I kept waving my arm. "Stop it!" she yelled.

I tried to respond, to say how everything medical brought me back to the worst days of my life – but couldn't connect the words to my tongue. My eyes grew wide. I couldn't remember how to speak! My face felt like fire and sweat trickled down my arms.

Snoopy nurse stepped back momentarily to admire her success at reapplying the tape, which allowed me to swivel one foot to the floor. I felt lightheaded yet had the second foot down. But was thwarted when the blue-smocked nurse injected something into the IV bag. She gently pushed me back, back, back.

A blessed calm slithered across my body. The pain softened – my eyelids grew heavy.

I started to drift – but couldn't shake two thoughts.

How did I get here?

And who exactly is Miss Barnett?

MORE TO COME WHEN
THE ONLY GIRL IN THE ROOM
ARRIVES IN 2025.

About the Author

 **Donna Y. Ferris** is a mother, rescue momma, and fintech executive with an MBA and CFA who mentors individuals to shape meaningful careers and lives. She holds an Inner MBA and career/life coaching, yoga therapy, and Reiki Master designations, hosts the "*Bounce Back Stronger*" podcast, and authored the memoir "*We've Got to Stop Meeting Like This.*" *Bounce Back Stronger* is a follow-up to that book.

Balancing career and home, Donna divides her time between West Chester, PA, Duck, NC, and Pittsburgh, PA – where her adult daughters and beloved Steelers live.

Donna leads workshops and retreats and speaks about resilience, writing, habit change, sobriety, and designing lives we love. She has also contributed articles and op-eds for the *Pittsburgh Post Gazette* and *Elephant Journal.*

Donna can be reached via email (donna@donnayferris.com) or on Facebook and Instagram (@donnayatesferris and @donnayferris, respectively) and on YouTube @donnayferris.

Printed in Great Britain
by Amazon